A Paines Plough and

C000121163

Long Time Dead

by Rona Munro

The first performance of
Long Time Dead
took place on 26 October 2006
at the Drum Theatre Plymouth

painesPLOUGH

DRUM THEATRE
PLYMOUTH THEATRES

ARTS COUNCIL ENGLAND

DRUM THEATRE

PLYMOUTH THEATRES

A Paines Plough and
Drum Theatre Plymouth Production

Long Time Dead
by Rona Munro

Cast *in order of appearance*

GNOME	Lesley Hart
GRIZZLY	Garry Cooper
DOG	Jon Foster
THE WIDOW	Jan Pearson

Director	Roxana Silbert
Designer	Miriam Buether
Lighting Designer	Chahine Yavroyan
Movement Director	Struan Leslie
Composer	Ben Park
Sound Designer	Richard Price
Assistant Director	George Perrin
Movement Director Assistant	Leonie Kubigsteltig

Production Manager	Nick Soper
Stage Manager	Julie Gilliam
Deputy Stage Manager	Judith Barrow
Sets, Props and Costumes	TR2 – Theatre Royal Plymouth
Costume Supervisor	Haldis Gothard

The playscript that follows was correct at time of going to press, but may have changed during rehearsals.

With special thanks to the Mount Batten Centre for all their advice, support and equipment.

GARRY COOPER (Grizzly)

Garry trained at the Drama Centre, London.

Theatre includes: Futures (Theatre 503), King Lear (ETT No 1 Tour & Old Vic), The Singing Group (Chelsea), The Mysterious Mother Loot, Chinchilla, What the Butler Saw, Macbeth, Orpheus (Glasgow Citizens), Doctor Faustus (Lyric, Fortune), Salonika (Royal Court), No Man's Land (Leicester Haymarket), Real Dreams, The Danton Affair (RSC).

Television includes: Heartbeat, Midsomer Murders, The Bill, Taggart, Doctors, Hiroshima, Charles II, Murder in Mind, Holby, Always and Everyone, At Home With The Braithwaites, The Vice, Dangerfield, Children of the New Forest, Dalziel and Pascoe, The Fix, No Bananas, Soldier Soldier, The Writing on The Wall, Against All Odds, Between the Lines, Perfect Scoundrels, Lovejoy, Men of the World.

Film includes: Harvest, Enemy of The Unseen, Jacob, The Emissary, Hostile Waters, Beautiful Thing, Quadrophenia, P'Tang Yang Kipperbang, 1984, Teddy Bears' Picnic, Walter, My Beautiful Laundrette, Pick Up Your Ears, Caravaggio, Mountains of The Moon, London Kills Me, An Ungentlemanly Act.

JON FOSTER (Dog)

Jon trained at East 15 acting school.

Theatre includes: Food (Traverse), After Haggerty (Finborough), A New Way to Please You, Speaking Like Magpies, Sejanus His Fall, Thomas More (RSC), Free from Sorrow (Tristan Bates), Romeo and Juliet (Creation), Jekyll and Hyde (Camden People's), Oliver Twist, The Melancholy Hussar (Etcetera), The Two Gentleman of Verona

(Pentameters), Treasure Island (Palace Theatre Westcliffe), Our Country's Good, Vinegar Tom (NHC), Brimstone and Treacle (Corbett).

Television includes: Instinct, Silent Witness.

Film includes: Still Moving, King Liam, Channel 5.

Radio credits includes: The Duchess of Malfi (BBC).

LESLEY HART (Gnome)

Lesley trained at the Royal Scottish Academy of Music and Drama.

Theatre includes: Strawberries in January (Traverse/Paines Plough), I was a Beautiful Day, Shimmer, Outlying Islands, Among Unbroken Hearts, Fireflies, Shetland Saga (Traverse), Elizabeth Gordon Quinn, Home - Aberdeen (NTS), Nightingale and Chase, A Midsummer Night's Dream, The Twits (Citizens), The Danny Crow Show (Dundee Rep), Tiny Dynamite (Paines Plough/Frantic Assembly/Lyric Hammersmith), Running Girl (Boilerhouse).

Television includes: Casualty, Panorama – Invisible Kids.

Radio includes: Almost Blue, Painting The Pope, 15 Minutes That Changed The World, Whoever You Chose To Love, The Golden Slipper, The Stranger At The Palazzo Dorro, Fifteen Minutes To Go, The Master of Balantrae, Bondagers (BBC Radio 4), Ghost Zone (BBC Radio 7), The Innocence of Radium (BBC Bristol), Himmler's Boy, Lynton Bay (BBC Radio Scotland).

JAN PEARSON (The Widow)

Theatre includes: Realism (Edinburgh Lyceum), Beauty & The Beast (RSC), Norman Conquests

(Theatre Clwyd), Angel Magick (Serious Music/ Albert Hall), Princess Sharon (Scarlet), The Jinx (Paines Plough/ Bridewell), Sabina (Bush), The Censor, Heredity, Tantamount Esperance, (Royal Court), Beauty and the Beast (Young Vic) Grimm Tales (Leicester Haymarket) and The Sisters (Scarlet).

Television includes: Silent Witness, Doctors, Where the Heart Is, Holby City, Cops, The Bill, Underworld, London Bridge, Inspector Wycliffe, The Chief.

Film includes The Invitation, Martha Meet Frank, Daniel and Laurence.

Radio includes: The Nationalisation of Women (BBC Radio 3), May and the Snowman (BBC Radio 4), Flowers of the Dead Red Sea (BBC Radio 3) and When it Comes (BBC Radio Wales).

MIRIAM BUETHER (Designer)

Miriam trained in costume design at Akademie für Kostüm Design in Hamburg and in theatre design at Central Saint Martins.

Theatre includes: pool (no water) (Drum Theatre Plymouth/Lyric, Hammersmith), Realism (National Theatre of Scotland), Unprotected (Traverse/Liverpool Everyman), The Bee (Soho Theatre), Trade (RSC/Soho Theatre), The Death of Kinghoffer (Edinburgh International Festival/Scottish Opera), After the End (Paines Plough/Bush), Way to Heaven (Royal Court), Platform (ICA), The Wonderful World of Dissocia (Drum Theatre Plymouth, Edinburgh International Festival, The Tron), Guantanamo (Tricycle, West End, New York), People Next Door (Traverse, Germany, Balkans, New York), The Dumb Waiter Oxford Playhouse), Bintou (Arcola, sitespecific), Red Demon (Young Vic, Bunkamura Tokyo), Eskimo Sisters (Southwark Playhouse),

Lebensspiele (Three Mills Island Studios, sitespecific).

Dance includes: Outsight (Fundação Calouste Gulbenkian, Lisbon), Tut (Theatre Maisonneuve, Montreal), Track (Scottish Dance), Body of Poetry (Komishe Opera, Berlin), Tender Hooks (Fundação Calouste Gulbenkian, Lisbon), Possibly Six (Maisonneuve, Montreal), 7DS (Sadler's Wells Theatre).

Awards include: 2004/2005 Critics Award for Theatre in Scotland, 1999 Linbury Prize for Stage Design overall winner, 1996 bursary of Carl Duisberg Gesellschaft.

STRUAN LESLIE (Movement Director)

Struan trained at London Contemporary Dance School and The Naropa Institute Colorado.

Theatre and opera (as Movement Director and Choreographer) includes: The Seagull, Fix-Up, Iphigenia at Aulis, Ivanov, The Oresteia (National Theatre), Les Negres (Freiburg, Germany),The Cricket Recovers, The Girl Of Sand (Almeida), Casanova (BBC/RED Productions), If Destroyed True (Paines Plough, Dundee Rep) Il Viaggio a Rheims, Marriage of Figaro (Stadt Theatre Opera, Germany),Jenufa, Cosi Fan Tutte (Welsh National Opera),Jephtha (Welsh National Opera/ENO), Katya Kabanova (Welsh National Opera/ Geneva),Iphigenia at Aulis (Abbey Theatre), The Country, Forty Winks (Royal Court), The Maids, Julius Caesar (Young Vic), Antigone (TAG), Slab Boys Trilogy, Solemn Mass for a Full Moon in Summer (The Traverse, Edinburgh, BITE). Oliver Twist (The Lyric Hammersmith),As You Like It, Merchant of Venice, Duchess of Malfi, Easter, Cyrano de Bergerac (RSC).

Theatre Direction includes: No (Sea) No (Gull) (National Theatre Platform), Carmen (WNO MAX), Spinning, 10,000 Broken Mirrors (Oval House)

Education posts include: Graduate Studies LABAN, London; International Council Visiting Professor, University of Illinois; Choreography and Movement, University Of Greenwich Education Faculty; Visiting lecturer, Faculty of Built Environment, South Bank University.

RONA MUNRO (Writer)

Rona is currently SAC Senior Playwriting Fellow for the Traverse Theatre.

Current projects include: an adaptation of Watership Down by Richard Adams (Lyric Hammersmith), The Indian Boy (RSC). Theatre includes: an adaptation of Mary Barton (Royal Exchange Theatre) and translation of Strawberries in January (Traverse/Paines Plough), Iron (Traverse/Royal Court), Fugue, Your Turn to Clean the Stair (Traverse), Snake (Hampstead Theatre), The Maiden Stone (Hampstead/Royal Lyceum), Gilt (Co-Writer), Bold Girls (Susan Smith Blackburn Award, Evening Standard Most Promising Playwright Award, Play International Award, Critics Circle and Plays and Players Most Promising Playwright Award), Saturday Night At The Commodore (7:84); The Way To Go Home (Paines Plough/Royal Court), Piper's Cave (Paines Plough/Boilerhouse).

Film includes: Ladybird Ladybird, Aimee and Jaguar.

Television includes: Rehab, Almost Adult.

Radio includes two of the plays in the latest Stanley Baxter Playhouse series for Catherine Bailey Ltd/BBC Radio 4.

BEN PARK (Composer)

Ben Park is co-Artistic Director of Walker Dance Park Music. He began producing music for Fin Walker's choreography in 1993 and has composed all of WDPM's music to date. He has extensive experience as a composer and musician, including touring with bands, composing for film, television, dance and theatre. His own music production company PARK MUSIC was established in 1996.

Recent commissions include: Shadow and The Journey (CandoCo Dance Company), Me & You (Phoenix Dance), The Truth (Ricochet Dance Productions), Reflection (Rambert Dance Company). In 2004 Ben Park was Composer-in-Residence at Opera North. Theatre includes: projects for the West Yorkshire Playhouse, Traverse, The English Shakespeare Company, Improbable Theatre and Indefinite Article's Dust, which won a Time Out Award in 2003.

Television includes: music for a BBC2 documentary series, for MTV and Channel 4 and Canterbury Tales, a BBC animated series which received, amongst other awards, a BAFTA and an Oscar nomination.

GEORGE PERRIN (Assistant Director)

George is the Trainee Associate Director at Paines Plough. He was the first recipient of the Genesis Directors Award at the Young Vic and is a member of the Old Vic New Voices company. George continues as Associate Director of nabokov, the new writing company he co-founded in 2001.

Theatre (as Director) includes: *Terre Haute* by Edmund White (Assembly Rooms, Edinburgh Festival) and *Camarilla* by Van Badham (Edinburgh Festival and Old Red Lion).

Theatre (as Assistant / Associate Director) includes: *After The End* by Dennis Kelly (directed by Roxana Silbert, National Tour, Moscow & New York), *Nikolina* by Van Badham (directed by James Grieve, National Tour) and *Tell Me the Truth About Love* by Rebecca Lenkiewicz (directed by Robert Delamere, Old Vic 24 Hour Plays).

ROXANA SILBERT (Director)

Roxana is Artistic Director of Paines Plough. She was Literary Director at the Traverse Theatre (2001-2004) and Associate Director, Royal Court (1998-2000). In 1997, Roxana was Associate Director of West Yorkshire Playhouse where she directed *Precious* by Anna Reynolds.

Theatre includes: Strawberries in January (Traverse/Paines Plough), Under the Black Flag (Shakespeare's Globe), Whistle In The Dark (Citizens), Damages (Bush), Property (NT Studio), Blonde Bombshells of 1943 (West Yorkshire Playhouse), The Slab Boys, Still Life from The Slab Boys Trilogy (Traverse/national tour), The People Next Door (Traverse/ Theatre Royal, Stratford East), Iron (Traverse/Royal Court), 15 Seconds, Greenfield, Quartz (Traverse), Brixton Stories (RSC), The Price (Octagon, Bolton), Almost Nothing and At the Table, I Was So Lucky, Been So Long, Fairgame, Bazaar, Sweetheart (Royal Court), Mules (Royal Court/Clean Break/ national tour), Splash Hatch on the E (Donmar Warehouse), A Little Fantasy (Told by An Idiot/London

Mime Festival), Top Girls, Translations (New Vic, Stoke), Cadillac Ranch (Soho), Write Away, Ice Station H.I.P.P.O (Channel 4 Sitcom Festival at Riverside Studios), Fast Show Live (Hammersmith Apollo/tour), The Treatment (Intercity, Festival, Florence).

Radio includes: Japanese Gothic Tales, Palm Life, The Tall One, The Taped Recorded Highlights of a Humble Bee (BBC Radio 4).

Television includes: Opera Lovers, Aphrodisiac.

CHAHINE YAVROYAN (Lighting Designer)

Chahine trained at the Bristol Old Vic Theatre School.

Theatre includes: Strawberries in January (Traverse/Paines Plough), When the Bulbul Stopped Singing, Outlying Islands, Iron, Green Field, Gagarin Way, Wiping My Mother's Arse; King Of The Fields, The Speculator, Danny 306 + Me (4 Ever), Perfect Days, Kill The Old Torture Their Young, Anna Weiss, Knives In Hens, The Architect, Shining Souls (Traverse). Other theatre credits include projects with companies and artists including: Bush, Crucible, Royal Court, Nottingham Playhouse, Leicester Haymarket, ICA, ENO, Lindsay Kemp, Rose English, Pip Simmons.

Dance includes: Yolande Snaith Theatredance, Bock & Vincenzi, Jasmin Vardimon, Anatomy Performance Company, Naheed Saddiqui. Site specific works include: Station House Opera, Dreamwork at St Pancras Chambers, Coin St Museum, City of Bologna, Italy New Year's Eve celebrations. Fashion shows for Givenchy, Chalayan, Clemens-Riberio, Ghost. He is also a long standing People Show Person.

'The legendary Paines Plough' *Independent*

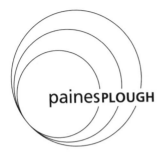
painesPLOUGH

Paines Plough is an award-winning, nationally and internationally renowned theatre company, specialising exclusively in the commissioning and development of contemporary playwrights and the production of their work for the stage.

Paines Plough has consistently commissioned the best writers of each generation. These include David Pownall, Stephen Jeffreys, Terry Johnson, Tony Marchant, Pam Gems, Mark Ravenhill, Sarah Kane, Abi Morgan, Gary Owen, David Greig, Philip Ridley, Douglas Maxwell, April De Angelis, Enda Walsh, Gregory Burke and Dennis Kelly. Currently we are producing an international tour of PRODUCT by Mark Ravenhill. In collaboration with Graeae Theatre Company we are producing *Wild Lunch*, a series of script-in hand lunchtime readings at the Young Vic Theatre in November.

Paines Plough has also developed a ground-breaking and pioneering programme of work aimed at building a new generation of theatre writers. We presently run *Later*, a unique late-night event at Trafalgar Studios in London's West End and *Future Perfect*, a year long playwriting programme for seven of the most exciting, daring and promising young British writers, as selected by Paines Plough and Channel 4 Television / Film Four. In order to inspire new playwrights and find new audiences, we also have a unique outreach programme which focuses on encouraging and enabling people of all ages, backgrounds and abilities to write for the stage.

In all its work, Paines Plough aims to challenge our notions of theatre and the society we live in.

Paines Plough is supported by

ARTS COUNCIL
ENGLAND

Paines Plough are

Artistic Director	Roxana Silbert
General Manager	Ushi Bagga
Literary Manager	Pippa Ellis
Administrative Assistant	Wojtek Trzcinski
Trainee Associate Director	George Perrin (Arts Council England)
*Associate Playwright	Enda Walsh (Arts Council England)
*Pearson Playwright	Katie Douglas
*Press Officer	Liz Smith (07971417210)

*Part-time staff

Board of Directors

Tamara Cizeika, Giles Croft, David Edwards (Chair), Chris Elwell (Vice Chair), Fraser Grant, Marilyn Imrie, Clare O'Brien, Jenny Sealey.

Contact

Wojtek Trzcinski, Paines Plough,
4th Floor, 43 Aldwych, London WC2B 4DN
T + 44 (0) 20 7240 4533, F + 44 (0) 20 7240 4534
office@painesplough.com
www.painesplough.com

THE PEARSON PLAYWRIGHTS' SCHEME

The Pearson Playwrights' Scheme awards five bursaries each year to writers of outstanding promise. Each award allows the playwright a twelve-month attachment to a theatre and commissions the writers for a new play. Previous recipients include Richard Bean, David Eldridge, Catherine Johnson, Charlotte Jones, Nick Leather, Martin McDonagh, Chloe Moss, Joe Penhall and Simon Stephens. Applications are invited via theatres in October of each year and judged by a high profile panel chaired by John Mortimer.

Katie Douglas is supported by the Pearson Playwrights' Scheme.

PEARSON

PLYMOUTH THEATRES

The Drum Theatre Plymouth has become a driving force in the South West and beyond, pioneering new forms of stage writing, physical theatre and other innovative work. As part of the Theatre Royal Plymouth complex, it has taken a leading role in an ongoing national exploration of new ways of producing and seeing theatre. In both 2002 and 2005 the Drum Theatre was nominated for the prestigious Peter Brook Empty Space Award.

The Theatre Royal's Young Company and People's Company have residency in the Drum Theatre, which also hosts extensive community and participation work. The Drum includes in its programme a network of leading national theatre companies – Graeae Theatre Company, ATC, Royal Court, Suspect Culture, Paines Plough, Half Moon, Red Shift Theatre Company, Travelling Light Theatre Company and Kesselofski and Fiske.

The Theatre Royal Plymouth is made up of the Theatre Royal itself and the Drum Theatre, as well as TR2, a new, innovative and award-winning Production and Education Centre housing the theatre-making processes, rehearsal facilities and extensive education, access and development activities.

A Note from the Artistic Director

We at the Theatre Royal have, in recent times, forged strong connections with Scottish theatre and Scottish playwriting and the Drum, bizarrely, is the proud possessor of a Critics Award for Theatre in Scotland. We've produced with Edinburgh's Traverse Theatre and the Edinburgh International Festival as well as Glasgow's Tron and that exciting ensemble, Suspect Culture. We've shown Plymouth new work by Anthony Neilson (The Wonderful World of Dissocia; Edward Gant's Amazing Feats of Loneliness), Isabel Wright (Mr Placebo) and, in conjunction with Paines Plough, Gregory Burke (The Straits)

Regardless of nationality, though, when offered the chance to produce a brand-new Rona Munro we naturally jump at it and, if it is to be directed by Roxana Silbert it is, as they say, a no-brainer. Rona's work is some of the most thoughtful and invigorating in the country and Roxana is, quite simply, a creative powerhouse.

With Long Time Dead, we are renewing a longstanding artistic collaboration with Paines Plough, who are no strangers to the South West and, under Roxana's new direction of this celebrated, writers' company, we hope to be working with them here often.

SIMON STOKES

Recent Productions

July 2004	**The Owl Service** adapted by Anita Sullivan and David Prescott from the novel by Alan Garner **Producer:** Drum Theatre Plymouth
September 2004	**The Wonderful World of Dissocia** by Anthony Neilson **Producers:** Drum Theatre Plymouth, Edinburgh International Festival, Tron Theatre Glasgow
October 2004	**Through A Cloud** by Jack Shepherd **Producers:** Drum Theatre Plymouth and Birmingham REP
February 2005	**Mercury Fur** by Philip Ridley **Producers:** Drum Theatre Plymouth and Paines Plough
May 2005	**Stoning Mary** by Debbie Tucker Green **Producers:** Drum Theatre Plymouth and Royal Court
September 2005	**A Brief History of Helen of Troy** by Mark Shultz **Producers:** Drum Theatre Plymouth and ATC
October 2005	**Presence** by Doug Lucie **Producer:** Drum Theatre Plymouth
February 2006	**The Escapologist** by Simon Bent **Producers:** Drum Theatre Plymouth, Suspect Culture and Tramway
May 2006	**NHS – The Musical!** by Nick Stimson and Jimmy Jewell **Producer:** Drum Theatre Plymouth
June 2006	**Pricked** by Anita Sullivan **Producers:** Drum Theatre Plymouth and Ripple
September 2006	**pool (no water)** by Mark Ravenhill **Producers:** Drum Theatre Plymouth, Frantic Assembly and Lyric Hammersmith
October 2006	**Long Time Dead** by Rona Munro **Producers:** Drum Theatre Plymouth and Paines Plough

Drum Theatre Plymouth
Royal Parade, Plymouth PL1 2TR
01752 267222
www.theatreroyal.com

Chief Executive	**Adrian Vinken**	Head of Workshop	**Tony Harvey**
Artistic Director	**Simon Stokes**	Head of Wardrobe	**Dina Hall**
Production and		Technical Co-ordinator	**Mark Hawker**
Technical Director	**Paul Clay**	Marketing Manager	**Marianne Smith**
Corporate Services		Press Offiicer	**Anne-Marie Clark**
Manager	**Paul Renyard**		(01752 230479)
Artistic Associate	**David Prescott**	Sales Manager	**Lynn Fletcher**
Acting Education &		Finance Manager	**Brenda Buckingham**
Arts Development		Theatre Manager	**Jack Mellor**
Manager	**John Whewell**	Catering Manager	**Angela Pawson**
Production Managers	**Nick Soper,**	Chair	**Councillor Nicky Wildy**
	David Miller	Vice Chair	**Peter Vosper**

LONG TIME DEAD

Rona Munro

Characters

GRIZZLY (Colin Ross), *mid- to late-forties, lowland Scots, from a mining family*

DOG (Jack Harrier), *mid-thirties, English*

GNOME (Naomi Miller), *early twenties*

THE WIDOW, *mid- to late-thirties*

OLD MAN / GHOST CLIMBER

Thanks to Drew, Panther, Joe, Alex and especially Mark.

This text went to press before the end of rehearsals, and may differ from the play as performed.

ACT ONE

On the Face of the Mountain

First we see the mountain, looming up into the sky, plunging down into an abyss, hanging over us. We hear a roar, a terrible roar of a storm that dies down to nothing but the panting of the three climbers, hanging in space, their head torches swinging wildly, giving off the only light apart from the all-pervasive glow of the sky reflecting off ice.

We are on an ice cliff, halfway down a mountain.

GNOME *is dangling, helpless, off a rope. She's injured, she can't move her arms and legs properly, she's bleeding. The middle climber, she's fallen below* GRIZZLY *and* DOG, *who are in the process of rescuing her.*

Their headlamps are flickering.

GNOME. I think I'm blind, Grizzly.

GRIZZLY. It's just blood in your eyes, darling. You're fine. We're nearly with you.

GNOME. Aw fuck . . .

GRIZZLY. Come on, Gnome, keep it together. I say Keith Richards. Has to be.

You hear that, Naomi?

GNOME *makes a strangled sound, struggling to move for a moment, and the ropes jerk between them.*

(*Sharply.*) Keep still, Gnome.

GNOME. Sorry . . .

GRIZZLY. OK. It's OK. Keith Richards is on the table. What do you say to Keith Richards?

GNOME. No.

DOG *is busy with the ropes, trying to get underneath* GNOME. GRIZZLY *is holding them both from above.*

GRIZZLY. The Gnome says no. Dog?

DOG. I agree with the Gnome.

3

GRIZZLY. The man *is* rock and roll. That is a rock and roll *life*.

DOG (*struggling to keep this going*). We trek fifty miles over snow and ice to the nearest human habitation. You say 'Keith Richards?' Nothing . . . Nada. Not a flicker, not a bootlegged CD. But . . . you say 'Michael Jackson?' . . .

GRIZZLY. Not rock and roll man, is it? Fame, yes. Music, no.

DOG. Not about the music. You didn't ask about the music. You said 'Who's the greatest rock and roll star of all time?' You think there's a news station in the world that hasn't had that white sunken face all over their screens?

GRIZZLY. Fame *and* music, that's what we're asking for . . .

DOG. They know his name in Papua New Guinea . . .

GRIZZLY. You been there? You asked anyone?

DOG. They know his name in Timbuktu . . .

GRIZZLY. Not for rock and roll . . .

DOG. Gnome, back me up.

GNOME. Elvis.

Pause as they let the weight of that sink in.

GRIZZLY. She's right.

DOG. Yeah. Point taken.

DOG *is braced next to* GNOME, *trying to clip her to him.*

GNOME. Ow! Ow, oh, it hurts, oh, Dog, it hurts.

DOG. Need to hold still, Gnomey.

GRIZZLY. Give us another one, Gnome.

GNOME *makes a sound of pain.*

Come on, Gnome, give us another one.

GNOME (*laughs*). OK. World's worst way to die.

GRIZZLY. You're sick. Always knew it.

GNOME. Come on.

GRIZZLY. No, give us another one.

GNOME. *Come on!*

GRIZZLY. This friend of mine fell downstairs and broke his neck and died and his family didn't notice. They thought he was pissed or having a laugh. They stepped over him for three days.

DOG. Don't believe it.

GRIZZLY. It's true.

DOG. Not saying it isn't true. Saying he wasn't a friend of yours. You read that in the paper.

GRIZZLY. Could still be friends of mine.

DOG. But would you admit to it, Grizzly. Would you boast about friends like that?

GRIZZLY. Just did.

DOG. Made it up. Disallowed. And it's not a bad death.

GRIZZLY. Breaking your neck is not a bad death?

DOG. Quick. Clean. You wouldn't even hear the snap.

GRIZZLY. Wrong.

DOG. That's a bit bald, isn't it? That's a bit sweeping. Wrong? What do you mean, 'wrong'?

GRIZZLY. Your brain stays functioning for about twenty seconds after everything else gets cut off . . .

DOG. You know that for a fact, do you?

GRIZZLY. Yeah, so you would hear the snap.

DOG. How the fuck could anyone know a thing like that?

GRIZZLY. They've seen people talking after they've been guillotined. Eyes rolling around, lips moving . . .

DOG. Who's seen? Who?

GNOME. It's true . . .

DOG. They make stuff like that up . . .

GRIZZLY. It was in a film . . .

DOG. Exactly!

GNOME. Still use guillotine . . . in France.

GRIZZLY. Do they?

GNOME. Yeah. That wins. Worst.

DOG. Why?

GNOME. 'Cause you can still see everything . . . after . . . head off . . .

GRIZZLY. Yeah!

DOG. What, they've interviewed some poor headless fucker? 'How do you feel?' 'Oooh I'm a bit light-headed but . . . '

He fakes death, head lolls.

GRIZZLY (*interrupting*). My worst way would be getting burned alive.

DOG *has finished righting* GNOME *and roping himself to her.*

DOG. OK, Grizzly.

GRIZZLY *starts to lower them to a ledge lower down.*

GNOME. Ow . . . fuck . . . ow . . . shit, Grizzly . . . No. Eaten by a polar bear, definitely, eaten by a polar bear while you're still alive.

GRIZZLY (*with effort*). Most dangerous animal on the planet.

DOG. So how come they're a fucking endangered species then?

GRIZZLY *is concentrating on lowering them slowly.*

GRIZZLY. Habitat. The ice is melting. Worse than sharks. I wouldn't want to be eaten by a shark either.

DOG. A tidal wave.

GRIZZLY. I had a friend who was eaten by a shark.

DOG. Real friend or someone you bonded with through newsprint?

They've nearly reached the ledge.

GRIZZLY. His name's Hector. I met him on the boats.

DOG. No one is really called Hector.

GRIZZLY. He had his leg half chewed off.

DOG. He deserves it with a name like Hector.

GRIZZLY. He said it just felt wrong.

DOG. Well, it's not going to feel good, is it?

GRIZZLY (*pausing for a moment, gathering strength*). Wrong. It didn't hurt, he said, not when it was happening. Just this feeling that something was happening to him that never should. A terrible dragging shaking feeling, he said, and he knew he had to stop it, and he knew he couldn't.

GRIZZLY *slowy lowers them down the last stretch to the ledge.* DOG *and* GNOME *are swinging in space.*

DOG. A cataclysmic volcanic explosion. That would be my worst.

GNOME (*painfully, with effort*). How did he stop it?

DOG. Do you want to know why?

They're on the ledge.

GRIZZLY. They reckon he hit it on the nose.

DOG (*tying them off*). Safe.

GRIZZLY *starts to climb down to them.* DOG *is securing* GNOME *to the wall.* GNOME*'s headlamp flickers and dies.*

GNOME. My light. Dog . . .

DOG. Don't worry. I can still see you, you look great. So I'm still saying a volcanic explosion.

GNOME. Why a volcanic explosion?

DOG. 'Cause you'd see the fucker coming and you'd think: 'OK. Maybe I can get above that, *maybe* it'll stop before . . . and then you'd see this wall of ash getting bigger, and bigger, and you'd know, there is no chance . . . and then it would hit . . .

GRIZZLY. But you wouldn't try and run away, would you?

DOG. Couldn't. That's why it's the worst.

GRIZZLY. I'd want to see it.

GNOME. Yeah. Me too. I'd want to see.

GRIZZLY *reaches the ledge.* GRIZZLY*'s light has also died.* GNOME *is pinned safely to the ice wall. She's in a lot of pain.*

DOG (*quietly to* GRIZZLY). What do you reckon?

GRIZZLY. We're nearly down, don't want to go further in the dark 'less we have to.

DOG. Sit it out here?

GRIZZLY. How bad is she?

GNOME. I'm great.

GRIZZLY. Good on you, Gnomey, just a little bit further in the morning, there'll be big smelly men with radios and a helicopter ride for all the good girls.

GNOME. Am I good?

GRIZZLY. Good enough. You've only fallen twice after all. Just don't make a habit of it.

GNOME. Have we got a worst one yet?

GRIZZLY. I heard this one the other day that I reckon is the worst . . .

GNOME. What's that?

GRIZZLY and DOG are pressing themselves round GNOME, sheltering her, trying to warm her, get food into her.

GRIZZLY. Get a kid, just a little kid, tell them they're going to die. Wait till they're old enough to understand it then tell them, let it sink in, then give them sixty or seventy years to think about it and watch it coming.

Pause.

DOG. You're being deep, aren't you?

GNOME. Yeah, you're right. That's the worst. We're not going to go like that, are we?

GRIZZLY. We're not living like that.

Abruptly GNOME starts to cry.

DOG. Woah! Tears alert.

GNOME. I wish you were my dad.

GRIZZLY. Darlin', what's this? Where did this come from?

GNOME. I do. I wish you'd always look after me.

GRIZZLY. I will, Gnomey.

GNOME. I wish you were my dad.

GRIZZLY. I am. I started early. I was only six years old but I saw your mother bending over the sandpit . . .

GNOME. No, you could be my dad! You're old enough.

GRIZZLY. Am I? Shit. Haven't you got a dad?

GNOME. Yes, but I like you better.

GRIZZLY. I'm never having kids. Empty your wallet, tear your heart out, follow you down the pub, banging on the door and asking you to come home . . .

GNOME. I won't! I promise. I'll be ever so good.

GRIZZLY. I can't handle the responsibility, pet. Tell you what,

I'll co-parent. I've fucked up this mountain and you're the result. Me and the hill. We'll have you.

GNOME. That's good. That's very good. I'm better now.

DOG. I don't want you to be my dad.

GRIZZLY. I wouldn't have you.

GNOME. You want to marry him.

GRIZZLY. It's true. I'm the only one who could make him feel like a real man.

DOG. Got to dream the dream, haven't you, Grizzly?

GRIZZLY. I know you do, Dog.

DOG. No, that would be a nightmare, Grizzly.

GRIZZLY. We are talking serious pain, I'll give you that. But you want it.

DOG. No, it would be like nudging me with a cashew, Grizzly.

GRIZZLY. We're talking python, mate.

DOG. Yeah? So when you look down . . . ?

GRIZZLY. At the length, yeah?

DOG. Whatever, can you see it? Looking down? Can you see it? Over the gut?

GRIZZLY. You know why I'm fat though, don't you? Every time I fuck your mother she gives me a pie.

GNOME. You love him more than me.

GRIZZLY. Who are you talking to now?

GNOME. Both of you. You do love him, admit it.

GRIZZLY. Is she getting serious and emotional?

DOG. I think she's trying.

GNOME. I'm allowed! I'm fighting for my life!

Throughout this GRIZZLY *and* DOG *are still working on* GNOME: GRIZZLY *warming her,* DOG *struggling on the tiny ledge to put up the bivvy tent.*

DOG. Oh listen to you, sixteen thousand feet up, a hole in your head, and a wind chill of minus twenty-five degrees degrees and you have to make a drama out of it.

GRIZZLY. Girls.

9

DOG. Moan, moan, moan . . .

GRIZZLY. That would be my girls. Your girls it's more yawn, yawn, yawn, isn't it?

DOG. I do wear them out, yes, Grizzly. The words 'Lethal Weapon'.

GNOME. Shut the fuck up!

DOG. Sorry, Gnome.

GNOME. Tell him you love him.

GRIZZLY. Why are you doing this?

GNOME. You guys have to keep climbing together. It's the most beautiful thing I've ever seen move over ice.

GRIZZLY. Is that my arse she's been staring up at or yours?

GNOME. Take this seriously! It's keeping me awake!

DOG. Fuck you. Nothing wrong with you.

GRIZZLY. Slap a bit of elastoplast on, you'll be fine.

DOG. Slap it on her mouth, what do you think?

GRIZZLY. Sounds good to me.

DOG. You know what it is?

GRIZZLY. What?

DOG. She thinks we've got a homoerotic subtext.

GRIZZLY. You've got a homoerotic subtext, mate. I've got the Kylie calendar, you bought the albums, and I don't think more needs to be said. Anyway, I'm still waiting for the woman of my dreams.

DOG. The blind one?

GRIZZLY. She will walk towards me out of the storm. And she'll look at me . . .

DOG. Flat on your back, drooling whisky . . .

GRIZZLY. Whatever, she'll look at me and she'll say . . .

DOG. I just love shagging fat men with no co . . .

GRIZZLY. No, no, that's later. First she'll say, 'Do you want to come into the warm? I've got a pepperoni pizza here.'

DOG. Aw fuck! That's *my* woman!

GRIZZLY. I saw her first.

10

DOG. No, right enough, mine's got macaroni cheese.

GNOME (*fading out*). Just tell him . . .

GRIZZLY (*sharply*). Woah, come on, Gnome, no slacking, eyes open.

GNOME. Tell him you love him.

GRIZZLY. Why?

GNOME. It would make me ever so happy.

DOG. All right. I'll tell you this. I wouldn't go up a hill with anyone else.

GRIZZLY. Might have to kill you now, Dog.

DOG. Sorry, man, just . . . you know . . . had to shut her up.

GRIZZLY (*to* GNOME). Happy now?

DOG. 'Course she's happy. Here she is, flat on her back, big man on either side of her. It's bringing back all sorts of precious memories, isn't it, Gnomey?

GRIZZLY. Hey!

DOG. What?

GRIZZLY. The Gnome is pure. The Gnome has never even kissed the back of her own hand.

GNOME. You don't know the half of it, Grizzly.

GRIZZLY. There are things a father should never know. The Gnome is dedicated to her art.

DOG. Whose arse?

GNOME. Oh no, I fucked up though, I fucked up.

DOG. Who did you fuck?

GNOME. I'm so sorry, guys. I'm so sorry.

GRIZZLY. Oh great, now she's delirious.

GNOME. You wanted this mountain so badly and I've messed it up.

GRIZZLY. Where's that elastoplast?

GNOME. It was such a stupid mistake . . . Just one stupid mistake.

GRIZZLY. Yeah, well there's always one stupid mistake. It was your turn.

11

GNOME. I'm so sorry.

DOG. It's nothing, a blow job each and we'll call it quits.

GNOME. I'm so sorry.

GRIZZLY. Record's stuck.

GNOME. I'm so sorry . . .

DOG. They never learn, do they?

GRIZZLY. Can't teach them.

DOG. I taught one to pick my socks up off the floor once.

GRIZZLY. How'd you do that?

DOG. Left them there till she got the hang of it.

GRIZZLY. You see, they're more intelligent than we give them credit for.

GNOME. Shut the fuck up! I hope your cock falls off!

DOG. That'd get an avalanche going.

GNOME. I'm serious. Enough of that.

GRIZZLY. Morning soon, Gnomey.

DOG. Soon as the light comes. We'll get moving.

GNOME. I don't want to die.

GRIZZLY. No one's going to die.

GNOME. But if I died here . . . I could live with it . . .

DOG. We'll let that go because you're a bit stressed.

GNOME. We'll be able to try again, won't we, Grizzly?

GRIZZLY. If we want. What does it matter? It's only a hill. Only a lump of rock.

DOG. We'll get it next time.

GNOME. I feel good now. I feel warm.

DOG *and* GRIZZLY *exchange worried glances. They move closer round* GNOME, *trying to share more body heat.*

GRIZZLY. Stay with us, Gnomey.

GNOME. I'm very happy.

GRIZZLY. We'll get through this night.

GNOME. Elvis will never die, will he?

GRIZZLY. Sacrilege to suggest it.

GNOME. No one will ever quite believe it. He'll live forever.

GRIZZLY. But was he happy?

GNOME (*slowing down*). Doesn't matter, he's a fucking demigod now, isn't he?

DOG. He's probably a aging loser flipping burgers somewhere. Elvis could hole up round here and no one would ever find him. Are you Elvis, Grizzly?

GRIZZLY. Tone deaf as it happens.

DOG. Stay with us, Gnomey. What's the first thing you're going to do when we get down?

GNOME (*groggy*). Get pissed.

GRIZZLY. That's the way to go.

Lights fade on them huddled on the icy ledge. GRIZZLY *and* DOG *still rubbing and rubbing at* GNOME's *hands and feet.*

The City

A quiet side street near a hospital. London, night.

GRIZZLY *is lying spreadeagled, as if he's dropped out of the sky. The* WIDOW *is looking at him.*

WIDOW. You're lying in the street.

GRIZZLY. Eh?

WIDOW. You're lying in the street. You have to get up.

GRIZZLY. Uh huh.

WIDOW. You're too heavy. I won't be able to lift you.

GRIZZLY. Hi there.

WIDOW. A car is going to run over your head.

GRIZZLY. Eh?

WIDOW. A car is going to run over your head.

GRIZZLY. Oh, OK.

He struggles to sit up.

That's fine, I'm all right.

GRIZZLY *still sits where he is, looking at his feet. He is only wearing one boot.*

WIDOW. You're still sitting in the road.

GRIZZLY (*looking at feet*). What the fuck . . .

WIDOW. You're still in the road!

GRIZZLY. I'm OK. I'm OK.

He gets to his feet and, hopping, limps out of the road.

WIDOW. I've been waiting for you.

GRIZZLY (*still looking at bootless foot*). What the *fuck* . . . ?

GRIZZLY *looks round for the missing boot.*

WIDOW. Your friend had to go.

GRIZZLY. Did he? Have you seen my boot?

WIDOW. I said I'd wait around. I was just on my way home.

GRIZZLY. Were you, darling? . . . I'm a bit pissed, to tell you the truth. Sorry.

WIDOW. You better come in.

GRIZZLY. Oh no, no, no.

WIDOW. Can you walk?

GRIZZLY. I wouldn't put you to any trouble. I seem to have lost my boot.

WIDOW. Come on.

GRIZZLY. Oh no. No, no darlin'. No. You're a sweetheart but you don't want to do that. I am a very big, very drunk man and it's dark. You're kind – god love you, you're kindness itself – but no. Don't go asking me in. I could be anybody and you're worth more than that.

WIDOW. This is a hospital. I'm a nurse.

GRIZZLY. Eh?

WIDOW. You need to come into A and E.

GRIZZLY. Aw, fuck that.

WIDOW. Suit yourself.

GRIZZLY. What am I doing here?

WIDOW (*peering at him closer*). I think you've probably been in a fight. Or you fell off something . . . or both.

GRIZZLY. Nothing hurts.

WIDOW. Wait till tomorrow. You probably need stitches.

GRIZZLY. Aw, fuck that. Sorry. You're very kind. You're very, very kind. I'll just have a wee sit down here, if that's OK.

WIDOW. I made a promise. I have to see you safe, you've got to . . .

GRIZZLY (*interrupting*). If it's not putting you out.

GRIZZLY *fumbles in his pocket for cigarettes. She watches for a moment then sighs impatiently and takes over getting out a cigarette for him, lighting it, passing it back.*

Kind. Very, very kind and probably beautiful. (*Peers at her.*) No too bad, anyway. Sorry, neither here nor there, how you look, irrelevant, you have a good heart. Worth its weight in rubies, a good heart. A man would be lucky to win a good heart even if the face looked like a slapped arse . . . Which it doesn't. What do you do?

WIDOW. I'm a nurse.

GRIZZLY. You see! You see, you're an angel. You gonna have a look at my head, it's nipping something desperate.

WIDOW. I just finished my shift.

GRIZZLY. Aye?

WIDOW. Oh, sod promises, break your heart every time.

GRIZZLY. Isn't that the truth? (*He offers his hand.*) Don't let the bastards grind you down.

She shakes his hand.

Good luck to you.

WIDOW. I'm going to have one of your cigarettes.

GRIZZLY. Help yourself, darling, what's mine is yours.

WIDOW. It's Colin, isn't it? Colin Ross.

GRIZZLY. Most people call me Grizzly.

WIDOW. What kind of name is that?

GRIZZLY. There's a story about a boy . . . Russian guy told me this, you'll like this . . . he has to climb up a glass mountain . . . Everyone wants to climb it, no one can climb it. I don't remember what's at the top, it's either a princess or treasure or both . . . anyway, the boy gets bear claws . . . and he ties them to his feet and hands . . . and he climbs up the glass mountain . . . He gets to the top. Isn't that a great story?

WIDOW. That's why you're called Grizzly?

GRIZZLY. No, no, no. Don't be daft. It's cause I'm fat, hairy and crabbit. (*Thinks.*) How'd' you know my name?

WIDOW. I met you. Earlier tonight.

GRIZZLY. You're a climber?

WIDOW. No. I'm a nurse.

GRIZZLY. So how did I meet you?

WIDOW. I was looking after your friend.

GRIZZLY. I need to get home. You got a minicab number, pet?

WIDOW. Have you got any money?

GRIZZLY *searches his pockets.*

GRIZZLY. Don't know that I do.

WIDOW. You've probably been robbed.

GRIZZLY. Bastards.

WIDOW. Where do you need to get back to?

GRIZZLY. The Pans.

WIDOW. Where?

GRIZZLY. You know, Prestonpans, just out of town.

WIDOW. Which town?

GRIZZLY. Edinburgh.

WIDOW. This is Southwark.

GRIZZLY. Eh?

WIDOW. You're in London. Look . . . (*Points.*) The Thames.

GRIZZLY *struggles to make sense of this but the effort's too much.*

GRIZZLY. Aw fuck.

WIDOW. I think you should go to the police, Colin.

16

GRIZZLY. Grizzly. It's Grizzly.

WIDOW. You should call the police.

GRIZZLY. Aw, fuck that . . . I need to get home.

WIDOW. Well, you can't walk it.

GRIZZLY. You're a really nice person, do you know that? I mean, you've probably saved my life.

WIDOW. Probably.

GRIZZLY. Which means you own it. I have to do anything you want now. What do you want me to do, angel?

WIDOW. I want you to go into A and E and get your head stitched up.

GRIZZLY. OK. OK. I'll just sit here a wee minute, if you don't mind.

WIDOW. You're getting too cold.

GRIZZLY. This isn't cold. I could tell you about cold . . . (*As realisation dawns.*) You know . . . you know, I'm not that pissed.

WIDOW. Really?

GRIZZLY. No serious, serious, something's coming back to me, I'm not that pissed, I'm just very tired . . . Why's that then?

WIDOW. Why is that?

GRIZZLY *thinks.*

GRIZZLY. No, Lost it. I need another boot. (*Remembering.*) Ah! It's OK! . . .

WIDOW. What is?

GRIZZLY. I'm supposed to be in London. The Gnome's in hospital here. Is this a hospital?

WIDOW. Yes.

GRIZZLY. Is she here?

WIDOW. Your friend. Yes.

GRIZZLY. The Gnome. Naomi.

WIDOW. She's here. I was looking after her. I met you.

GRIZZLY *peering.*

GRIZZLY. Doesn't look right. Don't remember this. How many fucking hospitals are there in London?

WIDOW. A lot.

GRIZZLY. You see, you're all sick down here. Now! I'm not drunk, well I am a bit drunk, but I'm not just drunk, I've not slept. Not on the hill, not on the plane . . .

WIDOW. Where have you been?

GRIZZLY. Well, up the second pitch but we didn't get near to the top. No, we didn't get to the top. A pin came out and the Gnome fell. One arm fucked, had to get her back. She held it together till we were nearly down then she fell again. And that was her head . . . kept talking through the night, trying to keep her with us . . . Wee thing. We were lucky to get her home safe. Getting too old for this.

Do I look like an old man to you?

WIDOW. Compared to who?

GRIZZLY. A proper old man. With wrinkly bits and no teeth.

WIDOW. You're lying in the road having a midlife crisis?

GRIZZLY. Three score years and ten, what's that?

WIDOW. Eh . . .

GRIZZLY. Seventy, it's seventy, the years of our lives are seventy so if I was having a midlife crisis I'd have to be more than . . . aw fuck . . .

WIDOW. What?

GRIZZLY. I thought it was eighty. That would be four score, wouldn't it? Even if it was . . .

Fuck, I'm more than halfway however you count it.

Still . . . modern medicine and that. You should know, you're a nurse, nearly everyone makes it past eighty, don't they, these days?

WIDOW. No.

GRIZZLY. Don't they?

WIDOW. No.

GRIZZLY. Some people make it to ninety! Some get telegrams from the queen!

WIDOW. Some do. Most don't.

GRIZZLY. You're a bit of a downer, do you know that?
Gnomey nearly died.

WIDOW. I'm sorry.

GRIZZLY. She's only twenty-two and she looks about nine.

Do you think I'll ever have kids?

WIDOW. I couldn't say.

GRIZZLY. Never worried about it. Plenty time . . . Plenty time.
I could have that, couldn't I? Kids. A seat by the fire in a
house. Why not? And if not that I can stop here for a few
years and wait for my boot. I'm a winner either way.

You see I'm a happy man.

I'm not fucking old yet.

WIDOW. Everyone's older than they were yesterday.

GRIZZLY. Everyone's a philosopher tonight. (*Trying to work it
out.*) The Gnome is bashed up in hospital, like a baby
mouse in cotton wool.

Dog and me got fucking legless. There was some bet . . .
couple of wankers with a Ford with a wind spoiler.

I may have lost the Dog somewhere . . .

WIDOW. Jack.

GRIZZLY. Who?

WIDOW. Is his name Jack?

GRIZZLY. The Dog, yeah.

WIDOW. He couldn't find you. He found me. I said I'd look
after you if I fell over you.

GRIZZLY. What happened to the Dog?

WIDOW. You got into an argument with two guys in the
waiting room. They didn't believe you were climbers. You
bet them everything in your wallet you could climb
anything in London and the three of you took off.

GRIZZLY. So what happened to the Dog?

WIDOW. You drew lots for who'd climb and who'd stay with
your other friend.

GRIZZLY. Aw, the Gnome. Is the Gnome OK?

WIDOW. She's doing very well.

GRIZZLY. Great. Good.

WIDOW. Do any of you have real names?

GRIZZLY. Real as anyone else's. (*Laughs.*) What a great night, eh? See, I could do that, eh? Make a living betting punters I could climb Big Ben. What a great night.

I'm so fucking broke, you know.

WIDOW. Are you?

GRIZZLY. All I've got is the money in my pocket . . .

Ooops.

WIDOW. I can lend you some.

GRIZZLY. No, no, no . . . See how good you are? Someone'll take advantage of that if you're no careful. (*Pause.*) There are stars up there but you can't see them. (*Pause.*) And the river is full of dark water. The river is flowing with inky, black water.

WIDOW. What are you on about?

GRIZZLY. Look around you!

The WIDOW *looks around her.*

WIDOW. Yes. Yes, I see.

GRIZZLY. It's a lovely mild night. A lovely mild night with a damp wind. Good for the trees, it'll clean their dusty leaves.

I hate sleeping in a house. Know why the Dog's called Dog? Because you can keep him in a house but it's never a great idea.

Bad for the upholstery.

WIDOW. Are you going to sleep here?

GRIZZLY. No one'll bother me. I've only got one boot.

WIDOW. I don't think that's safe.

GRIZZLY. What's safe?

Pause.

WIDOW. Come back inside and let me patch you up.

Pause.

GRIZZLY. Well, that's definitely not safe. My mother told me never to go off with strangers.

WIDOW. I'm a nurse.

I'll feed you. I'll wash your wounds. I'll patch you up and keep you warm.

GRIZZLY. Why would you do that?

WIDOW. You made me see the sky.

GRIZZLY. Yeah but . . . I couldn't give you anything else.

WIDOW. I promised your friend. And I don't really want to go home tonight.

GRIZZLY. I think I should sleep here.

WIDOW. I think you should come with me. The residents have left half a pepperoni pizza in the nurses' kitchen.

GRIZZLY. Ah well. (GRIZZLY *struggles to his feet.*) That's settled then.

Inside the hospital

GRIZZLY *singing in the darkness, 'You were always on my mind.'*

Lights up on GRIZZLY *and the* WIDOW. *He sits very close to the* WIDOW *in a small, dark, intimate space. She is bathing his wounds.*

Everything is white. GNOME *is in a bed close by. She's in a room next door or at the other end of the ward. She's close but* GRIZZLY *can't see her. She is shielded by white screens, bandaged, attached to drips. She is unconscious.*

GRIZZLY *finishes singing. He is now pretty much sober.*

GRIZZLY. You like that one?

WIDOW. Yes.

GRIZZLY. He just lived too long, didn't he? Too long or not long enough. But he had it. He had the real thing. No one can take that away from him.

WIDOW. If he'd had the self respect to stick to a diet he'd be alive today. He was lost.

GRIZZLY. Was he fuck. He had 'Jailhouse Rock' and 'Heartbreak Hotel' . . . Doesn't matter what he did after that. He'd done enough. He just ate too much crap.

21

WIDOW. Yeah. And it killed him.

GRIZZLY. Anything could kill you. We're all only here for the blink of an eye. Might as well taste the sugar.

Pause.

WIDOW. I haven't smoked for years. My head's spinning.

GRIZZLY. We all need a wee bit of excitement.

WIDOW. It's not excitement, it's self-inflicted punishment. I favour dodgy shags myself.

GRIZZLY. Oh, darling, no, I'm no good to you tonight.

WIDOW. No . . .

GRIZZLY. We could give it a go but I'd be astonished.

WIDOW. No. I'm just going to sew your head up.

GRIZZLY. And that's not you talking. You're better than that. You've really got something.

WIDOW. What?

GRIZZLY. I don't know . . . I'm thinking of the word . . .

WIDOW. Hold still.

GRIZZLY. Is that sterile?

WIDOW. Bit late to get picky.

GRIZZLY. You've no just been sewing fucking buttons on with that, have you?

WIDOW. I don't sew on buttons. I'm too busy sewing up drunks.

GRIZZLY. Concentrated, that's the word.

WIDOW. What for?

GRIZZLY. For you. You're like orange squash, you're cask strength whisky, have to dilute you before you could stand it.

WIDOW. Is that supposed to make me feel good?

GRIZZLY. I think that'd feel very good, if a man was living dangerously.

WIDOW (*sewing his head*). Hold still.

GRIZZLY. I can't feel that at all. Is that bad?

WIDOW. You've got a few more scars up here, haven't you?

GRIZZLY. I'm practically a fucking pirate.

WIDOW. I've got no head for heights myself.

GRIZZLY. I'll let you into a secret. I'm not crazy about them either.

WIDOW. So how do you climb?

GRIZZLY. Carefully.

Could you get into trouble for sorting me out like this?

WIDOW. The wait in A and E's eight hours at the moment. I'll be back on shift by then. Might as well look after you now. We've got different rules up here, anyway.

GRIZZLY. Different rules at the top.

WIDOW. Last station on the line.

GRIZZLY. Why are you sorting me out?

WIDOW. Maybe I thought you needed intensive care after all.

GRIZZLY. See, you are fucking coming on to me! OK, I'm a bit drunk but I know you're coming on to me!

WIDOW. You wish.

GRIZZLY. I would be very happy. I make no apologies for that. Just don't say all that rubbish about . . . dodgy shags and that . . . that's not you talking.

WIDOW. I'll tell you something. You don't want to take the smell of it home to the kids, and that says it all.

GRIZZLY. You got kids? Who's looking after your kids?

WIDOW. My sister.

GRIZZLY. So who's at home for you? Who are you living with?

WIDOW. My sister.

GRIZZLY. In with a chance then.

WIDOW. Yeah, my sister's not too fussy. Hold still. (*Pause.*) You were sweet. With your friend.

GRIZZLY. Yeah?

WIDOW. The way you were talking to her . . .

GRIZZLY. Well, someone said she might be hearing it.

WIDOW. I said. The things you were telling her . . . I thought you had a good heart.

GRIZZLY. I like puppies too. I'm practically marriage material.

WIDOW. But you're not?

GRIZZLY. Oh, fuck no.

No, no, no, no, no.

Pause.

Are you married?

WIDOW. I was married.

GRIZZLY. What happened to him?

WIDOW. He died.

GRIZZLY. So you're a widow?

WIDOW. I'm a widow.

GRIZZLY. I don't think I've ever met a widow apart from my mum.

Aw shit, am I being tactless now?

WIDOW. I don't mind. It's my wedding anniversary today actually.

GRIZZLY. How did he die?

WIDOW. He walked in front of a bus.

GRIZZLY. Serious!?

WIDOW. Yes.

GRIZZLY. On purpose!?

WIDOW. I'll never know.

GRIZZLY. *Serious!?*

WIDOW. Yes.

It's OK. It was years ago now.

GRIZZLY. My brother died years ago. And that's not OK. It's never that OK, is it?

WIDOW. How did your brother die?

GRIZZLY. Up the hill.

WIDOW. What hill?

GRIZZLY. The one me and the Gnome and Dog have just come home from.

Pause.

We didn't get to the top that time either.

Pause.

WIDOW. I didn't think there were any unclimbed mountains left?

GRIZZLY. Aw, there's loads. Lot of them you can't get at. Lot of them are too dull to bother with. This one isn't unclimbed anyway. There's been at least ten ascents since the seventies. But not the way we were going, which, no that I'm bragging, is the real come and have a go if you think you're hard enough way to *go*.

WIDOW. What I don't understand is why you would you want to risk your lives . . .

GRIZZLY (*interrupting*). We weren't risking our lives. We're no stupid. We're here, aren't we? Motorways are more dangerous.

Gnome just made a wee mistake. Bless her.

WIDOW. OK, why would you want to go through all this to get to the top of a mountain a dozen other people have climbed already?

GRIZZLY. Because I've no climbed it.

Pause.

WIDOW. You know, I like obsession. I just don't understand it.

GRIZZLY. Who's obsessed? I'm no obsessed.

WIDOW. What do you do for a living?

Pause.

GRIZZLY. Ah, fuck off.

WIDOW. What?

GRIZZLY. I run a climbing shop.

WIDOW. Really? And who's looking after business?

GRIZZLY. Business is not great.

WIDOW. I'm not surprised if you're taking three month holidays to climb mountains.

GRIZZLY. It's seasonal work! That's the point.

WIDOW. If you say so.

She finishes sewing him up.

There. All done.

GRIZZLY *touches his head. He winces.*

GRIZZLY. Aw, God that hurts now. Is that good?

WIDOW. That's good. You're starting to regain normal reactions.

GRIZZLY. Well, isn't that boring? Are you going to kick me out now?

WIDOW. I'll make you some coffee, then I should get home. I'm pushing a favour as it is.

GRIZZLY. Stay with me.

WIDOW. No.

GRIZZLY. Stay with me.

WIDOW. Why?

GRIZZLY. You'll like it. It'll be dead romantic.

WIDOW. What? Watching you sleep?

GRIZZLY. I'm past sleeping. I'm waking up again.

How long's he been gone?

WIDOW. Why do you want to talk about that?

GRIZZLY. It's 3.a.m. It's the time of night you think about the dead.

WIDOW. It's the time of night people die. Between three and four.

GRIZZLY. Are there folk dying here? Right now?

WIDOW. Maybe. Only people we've decided we can't stop slipping over. There'd be alarms going off otherwise.

GRIZZLY. My dad died in hospital.

WIDOW. Most people do.

GRIZZLY. He was a miner. Choked to death in a strange bed. He was fifty-seven.

WIDOW. What did he think of your career choice?

GRIZZLY (*grinning*). Ah . . . those weren't the best father son chats we ever had. Pete, my brother, actually did a year down the pits. But then there were no pits so what the fuck,

26

might as well be up a mountain. Pete got the hammering off Dad, I just got the bitter disappointed stare. Pete broke the trail on that one.

WIDOW. He was older than you?

GRIZZLY. Two years. Sometimes folk took us for twins. 'Course, I'm the good-looking one.

He slept in the bed next to me for years and talked to me in his sleep. 'Col . . . Col you wee shite, where you going?' I was right by him. Thought I was running away with his socks. That was his dream every night. Cold feet dream. (*Showing his hands*.) See my fingernails? Those are his fingernails. Exactly.

You just knew he was there for you? You know? Grinning.

Everyone says I'm so like him.

So I miss him but they don't have to.

Didn't climb for two years after I lost him.

WIDOW. When did you lose him?

GRIZZLY. Fifteen years ago last Friday.

That was the day we were supposed to be on the top this time.

WIDOW. How did he die?

GRIZZLY. We made a mistake. We didn't look at the weather.

Pause.

WIDOW. You know, when you've lost someone . . . there's a time when you've done the grieving. You've got over the days where the pain is just raw and red and there where your skin should be. You've learned not to think about it all the time. You've got on with your life. You've got over it . . . And then one day you think, OK, I've been good, I've dealt with this, I'm getting on with my life, when do I get my reward? When does he come back? And you realise he's never coming back.

GRIZZLY. I still think I see him up there sometimes. If I'm tired, I think he's ahead of me, like he always was. I look for the line . . . and I'm expecting to follow his lead.

WIDOW. The kids hardly remember him.

Pause.

GRIZZLY. I would quite like to kiss you about now.

WIDOW. Why?

GRIZZLY. I don't know.

Shut you up maybe? Cheer you up?

Pause.

Don't you fancy it?

Pause.

WIDOW. That's not something I can do now.

GRIZZLY. How about a cuddle then? Could you manage that?

Pause. The WIDOW *moves to him. They hold each other gently, tenderly, for a long time.*

WIDOW. You should sleep. There's a bed through there. You can lie down.

GRIZZLY. Will you lie down with me?

WIDOW. I'll look in on you.

GRIZZLY. Och well . . . that's a start.

She leads him off.

From the darkness there is the sound of painful, laboured breathing. An OLD MAN *appears at one side of the stage in a hospital gown, dragging a drip. He makes slow, painful progress across the stage, dragging the drip behind him and vanishes into the darkness on the other side.*

GRIZZLY *is back on. An hour has passed.*

He goes to GNOME. *He picks up her unconscious hand.*

Can't sleep, Gnomey.

Gnomey? . . . You're going to be all right. Did you hear me before? You're going to be all right. Don't tell anyone, but I've fixed it. I'm going to make a deal. I'm going to quit. See? See how that works? No more mountains. Never have to do another mountain. I won't bother them and they won't bother me and mine. And you'll be safe. See how that's going to work?

Gnomey? Can you hear me? If you can hear me, darlin', you can't ever tell anyone I said that 'cause it's fucking insane.

I want to do that for you, darlin'.

And it's time.

This is the deal. I'll say I'm giving up, for all the universe to hear. The minute I say it, and I mean it, Gnomey'll wake up. That's the deal I'm offering. You all hear me?

Out of the darkness comes the sound of laboured breathing.

GRIZZLY *gets up and goes to look.*

The OLD MAN *in a hospital gown is coming back the other way very, very slowly, still dragging a drip stand. As* GRIZZLY *watches he inches his way along the length of the ward or corridor, fighting for every breath.* GRIZZLY *doesn't say anything until the* OLD MAN *draws level, seemingly mesmerised by the sight, then he makes an awkward half move towards him.*

Do you want a hand there, pal?

The OLD MAN *does not turn his head or give any sign he's even heard* GRIZZLY. *He inches on into the darkness again and vanishes.*

GRIZZLY *looks where he's gone for a moment then he takes his mobile out of his pocket and punches a number.*

Fuck man, I've just seen a ghost.

Behind him DOG *appears at the open window of* GNOME's *room. He's climbed up the exterior wall. He's talking into his own mobile, neither of them see each other.*

DOG. Whose ghost?

GRIZZLY. I don't know, last seen at 7,000 metres badly needing oxygen. Where are you?

DOG. I'm at the hospital, where the fuck are you?

GRIZZLY. *I'm* at the hospital! Where the fuck are you?

DOG. I'm with the Gnome.

GRIZZLY. *I'm* with the Gnome . . . (*Turning.*) Where are . . . ? (*Sees* DOG, *doubles up laughing.*) What are you doing?

They're both still talking on their phones even though they're only a few feet apart.

DOG. They wouldn't let me in this time of night. Someone has to keep an eye on the Gnome.

GRIZZLY. *I'm* keeping an eye on the Gnome.

DOG. You weren't last time I looked, you were halfway up this wall in very poor style and then you . . .

The WIDOW *is running out of the dark, at* GRIZZLY.

WIDOW (*hissing whisper*). *No!*

The DOG *ducks back out of sight.*

GRIZZLY. What?

WIDOW. No mobiles! You're not allowed mobiles in here! Can't you read?

GRIZZLY. I'm dyslexic.

WIDOW. OK, big red signs with a picture of a . . .

GRIZZLY. How about going out, eh? How about like dating?

Pause.

WIDOW. I don't date. I work nights and I've got kids.

GRIZZLY. Brilliant. How old?

WIDOW. Ten and thirteen.

GRIZZLY. You know that thing you see in adverts, when your kid's got a cold and you come into the room after they're asleep and watch them breathing. Do you really do that?

WIDOW. Yes, you really do that.

GRIZZLY. That's brilliant. I'd love to see that. Let's do that.

The drink thing I mean.

WIDOW. All right.

GRIZZLY. All right?

WIDOW. I'll think about it.

GRIZZLY. Great. (*Of the* GNOME.) I'm OK to sit with her a bit longer?

WIDOW. I'll tell the next shift.

GRIZZLY. Thank you. I'll see you tomorrow?

WIDOW. Yes.

GRIZZLY. Great.

The WIDOW *hesitates for a moment then she leaves again.*

GRIZZLY *crosses to the window and helps* DOG *into the room.*

I've just made a date. I think I'm in love.

DOG. Serious? You asked her out?

GRIZZLY. Yeah.

DOG. Is she a psychiatric nurse?

GRIZZLY. Where the fuck have you been?

DOG. Looking for you.

GRIZZLY. I'm right here.

DOG. You weren't. You were halfway up this wall here and
then you came off.

GRIZZLY. Ah.

DOG. Yes.

GRIZZLY (*touching his head*). That explains it.

DOG. I hung on for a bit but then you never came back. Far as
I knew you were still lying down there. Had to go and look.
Nothing. Not even a dent in the ground.

GRIZZLY. Think I might have wandered off.

DOG. So I suppose we didn't win the bet?

GRIZZLY. Those bastards! They cleaned me out. I think I had
to hammer them. They took my wallet, Dog!

DOG. I've got your wallet, man. You gave it to me to keep safe.

GRIZZLY. Well, hand it over you thieving wee shite.

DOG *hands him his wallet.*

DOG (*of the* GNOME). How's she doing?

GRIZZLY. I don't know, man.

They both consider the GNOME *in silence for a moment.*

DOG. She looks about ten years old.

GRIZZLY. Great wee climber.

DOG. The best.

GRIZZLY. I don't get it. Why did they say it was safe to fly
her out if it wasn't safe to fly her out?

DOG. God, how're they going to know? Head injuries.
(*Pause.*) We flew over the thing, did you see?

GRIZZLY. What was it looking like?

DOG. Perfect. The whole face was shining white under the
moon. Firm band of black rock just pointing the way to that

sharp summit. It was a beautiful night. Just right. We'd've made it that night.

GRIZZLY. Well. It wasn't that night.

DOG. We'll get it next year.

GRIZZLY. Or whenever. No rush.

DOG. Got to be next year. Can't wait. I'm hot for it now. Bastard thing.

GRIZZLY *says nothing. He crosses to the window and looks out.*

GRIZZLY. Fucking concrete's sheer! How'd you do that?

DOG. Well, if you could see, I wouldn't have to lead half the pitches we ever climb, would I?

GRIZZLY (*sees something*). Ah!

DOG. What?

GRIZZLY. That's a crack.

DOG. Oh yeah, you see it now.

GRIZZLY. That's why you picked that wall! Easy peasy fucking crack only a poor old drunk.

DOG. We picked that wall because you can't see it from the road and there's hardly any windows looking out over it. You probably scared some poor woman in obs and gyny into premature labour but apart from that we got away with it.

GRIZZLY. That is fucking madness, whose idea was it to make a bet like that?

DOG. You were up for it!

GRIZZLY. Aw, Dog man, I've got to stop doing shite like this.

DOG. Why?

GRIZZLY. You went to look for me . . . and then you had to have a go at the wall?

DOG. Breezed it. What?

GRIZZLY. I canny keep this up.

DOG. Shut the fuck up, get some sleep, have a go yourself when the light's better.

GRIZZLY. No way am I . . .

DOG. Shut up, I'll rope it for you then, just shut up.

DOG lights up a fag and leans out the window with it.
Shares it with GRIZZLY, looking up at the night sky.

I hate looking at that.

GRIZZLY. What?

DOG. City skies. Clear night and no stars.

GRIZZLY. They're still there.

DOG. Beautiful clear night. But you can't see the stars. Street glow, just the moon and seven-four-sevens.

GRIZZLY. You'll see real stars again. You know, that is a fuck of a crack. It's got to make you worry about the state of the health service.

DOG. I hate hospitals.

GRIZZLY. They always put the serious wards right on the top, don't they? Closer to the sky.

Pause.

DOG. It's the smell. I hate the smell.

In the bed GNOME makes a small movement, a faint noise.
They go straight to her.

GRIZZLY. Gnomey?

DOG. Are you with us?

GRIZZLY. How're you doing, darlin'?

GNOME is still unconscious.

DOG. Aw, wake up, Gnomey, please . . . (*Whispering.*) Please.

GRIZZLY. Her brother's coming tomorrow.

DOG. We're going to stay with her though.

GRIZZLY. All the way. The Gnome is going to get through this. The Gnome is going to be all right.

DOG. I know she is. I know.

Pause.

How high did you and Pete get, anyway?

Pause.

GRIZZLY. Just below the rock band.

DOG. It would've been plain sailing.

GRIZZLY. Yeah.

DOG. Have we done everything you and Pete climbed now?

GRIZZLY. Yes. Yes we have.

DOG. Thought so.

Pause.

Maybe this isn't the time . . .

GRIZZLY. What for?

DOG. I had some ideas. For next year. After we've knocked off that bastard hill of course. Do it for Gnomey . . . with Gnomey . . .

GRIZZLY. We can talk to her.

DOG. Yeah?

GRIZZLY. They say she might hear. They say it might help.

DOG *looks back at* GNOME, *uncertain.* GRIZZLY *is finally slowing, exhaustion catching up with him. He's falling asleep.*

DOG. I fancied Janak Himal, what do you reckon? I heard someone was getting sponsorship together to make a push on a few round there. Could find out who, tag along, do our own thing on the side as per . . . What do you reckon?

Medical alarms go off somewhere in the darkness, the sound of hurrying feet, hushed, urgent voices.

(*Freaked.*) What the *fuck?*

GRIZZLY (*barely registering*). Someone slipping over that's no supposed to go yet.

DOG. I hate hospitals.

GRIZZLY. I'm going to have a wee nap, Dog, you all right for a bit?

DOG. Yeah, yeah . . . I'm fine.

GRIZZLY. Listen man, I need to give this up soon.

DOG. Give what up?

GRIZZLY. Fannying about up hills.

Pause.

DOG. For how long?

GRIZZLY. Well . . . forever. I need to give up for good.

Pause. Then the DOG *laughs and points at him 'Good one!'*

No, really.

DOG. Really?

GRIZZLY. Aye.

DOG. But . . . what'll you do?

GRIZZLY. I don't know. Have a real life.

DOG. What's that?

GRIZZLY. I don't know. Pub lunches, gardens . . . kids.

Pause.

DOG. It'll be OK, Grizzly. Gnome's going to make it. You said so.

GRIZZLY. It's no just that. This fucking shoulder is still stiff, four days off the hill and I still can't . . . (*Trying a tricep stretch, failing.*) See you do it.

DOG *does.*

There you go. Right there. Middle-aged fucking sinews.

DOG (*idea*). Yoga! I know this guy . . .

GRIZZLY. Get tae . . . My day's done, Dog.

Pause.

DOG. But . . . who would I go up with?

GRIZZLY. Anyone you like, man! They'll be fighting over you, come on.

DOG. You've been thinking about this for a while, haven't you?

GRIZZLY. Aye.

DOG. Gnomey smelt it, didn't she? I thought you were just a bit down, being on that hill . . . remembering Pete . . .

GRIZZLY. Maybe. Anyway. That's what I'm thinking. So are we OK?

DOG. Yeah . . . course man.

They're really really not but it hardly shows.

GRIZZLY. Good.

And I'm always remembering Pete.

Pause.

DOG. Yeah, yeah, yeah . . . I know. (*Pause.*) I think I saw him, Grizzly.

Pause.

GRIZZLY. Who?

DOG. Pete.

It was just before Gnomey came off the first time. Just below the rock band.

GRIZZLY *sits up and looks at him.*

What colour was his jacket?

Was it blue?

GRIZZLY. Where?

DOG. I was waiting for the Gnome and I looked west along the face. There was this flash of colour . . . about twenty metres away, a ledge and this shape on it, sort of slumped. I tried to get the torch steady on it . . . And it looked like it was someone . . .

He was on the ledge, looked like he was just sitting there.

Then Gnome came off.

Pause.

GRIZZLY. You should have told me.

DOG. We were busy.

GRIZZLY. Yeah. Yeah we were.

DOG. Maybe I shouldn't have told you at all. I didn't know what to do for the best.

I mean nothing's certain, man. There was that Japanese expedition in 98, they lost a guy, didn't they?

GRIZZLY. Think so.

DOG. So who knows?

GRIZZLY. Can't be sure.

DOG. No.

Pause.

You all right?

GRIZZLY *says nothing.*

DOG (*quietly*). You still awake, man?

GRIZZLY. Yes.

I'm fine. Can't think about it now. Need sleep.

Pause.

DOG. Can't believe you asked that nurse out?

GRIZZLY. She's good.

DOG. Is she? You really like her?

GRIZZLY. She's a reason . . . to close my eyes.

DOG. You should ask her the million dollar question then.

GRIZZLY. What's that?

DOG. Do you mind if I stick my ice axe in your hall cupboard?

GRIZZLY. I'll do that.

DOG. See that you do. (*Pause.*) Grizzly? Grizzly, you awake, man?

No answer. DOG *fidgets restlessly. He picks up the* GNOME*'s hand again.*

(*Quietly.*) Hey, Gnomey. Me again. Dog. Can you hear me all right? You're looking good. Really. You're looking . . .

Anyway . . .

Still dark.

You need to wake up and get out of this place, Gnomey. I don't think it's good, I don't think it's good for you being here. Need to get your shit together and get your boots back on, girl. Lazy. That's what I call it lying in bed all this time . .

So . . . I'm a bit peckish but there's no vending machines. Don't think chocolate and intensive care are supposed to go together. What do you think? You're not really holding up your end of the conversation, Gnomey. Not that I'm sensitive or anything . . .

So you need to . . . you know . . . get up . . . get back out there. (*Idea.*) Yeah! Where do you want to go, Gnomey?

Where do you reckon? Because you're no trouble. You can definitely come along again in case you're worried that your total fuck up has put anyone off. Just show a bit of energy here, you know like getting your eyes open, little things like that and, you know, you're in . . . All you've got to do is ask.

When you open your eyes, the first thing you'll see will be Grizzly's big ugly mug, so you don't scream, right? You don't scream. You say 'When are we going up the hill, Dad?' Try it for me. You say it. 'When are we going up the hill, Dad?' You say it . . . OK, maybe later. (*Pause.*) I went up Glencoe in a painter decorators van with only three working gears . . . Painting decorating was for cash, you know, not even pretending it was a career path. I tell you what an education gets you, Gnomey, a life behind double glazing, no way was I suffering that, the family's beyond despair at this point. . . . I didn't even know where I was going, just that you were supposed to go there . . . where the mountains were . .

Well, you know . . . You know what that view's like. Hills for heros . . . and there was no one there but old men and scramblers in Aran knits . . . fucking disappointment . . . Went up with this old dear . . . taking five minutes putting a stopper knot on every fucking thing . . . took so long on his lead I smoked half a pack and then I couldn't fucking take it, unroped and soloed past him, left him to it. But he'd made me late, there's a cloud on the sunset before I get to it, he'd robbed me of the view, Gnomey.

And he wasn't happy, oh fuck he wasn't happy about that . . . I'm sleeping in the van but I'm drinking in the Clachaig . . . fucking High Noon, tumbleweed blowing through conversations when I walk in . . . and I'm going round the tables trying to get myself someone else on the rope to have a go at Orion Direct in the morning. I didn't have a clue. I just knew it was hard . . . Leprosy . . . they think they'll catch something from breathing the same air as me . . . no one'll even look me in the eye . . . 'cept this keg covered in fur . . . He's looking at me, like he knows me, like he's thinking about something, like he's making his mind up but he doesn't speak . . . then Mr Stopper Knot pipes up . . . 'He'll kill you, Grizzly.' And straight away Grizzly says 'Let's give it a go then.' We went for it in the morning and I couldn't keep up. Drove me insane like a rat eating my guts, watching him dance over a pitch and I couldn't even see how he pulled it off, I just had to follow.

Didn't say another word to me till we were nearly up there, pumped out, hanging back on the ropes. Then he says, 'If you fancy doing this again sometime, I'm game.'

So we did.

They told me afterwards he hadn't climbed for two years before that day. Not since Pete went.

But he must have been waiting in the bar for somebody, eh Gnome? Or why was he there?

Our first climb, ice and grey rock, warm and fluid under your fingers, ravens flying under your boots. Clear sky and the sparkle hitting the lochs and the hills, holding light in their laps, holding the clouds for you to look down on.

See it, Gnomey? Remember? You're up there.

Right at the end of this speech the WIDOW *creeps in and lies down in the bed with* GRIZZLY, *wrapped around him.*

Got to get up there . . .

DOG *falls silent for a moment, remembering, looking past* GNOME *at the window.*

(*Getting up.*) Going to get a look at the sky, Gnomey, back soon.

DOG *leaves. A lighting change, it's dawn, weeks later.* GRIZZLY *is talking as if he's just picking up the story from* DOG.

GRIZZLY. And when you're up there. And it's just one foot in front of the other. Going up or coming down. Just one foot in front of the other and making your legs move, making your hands work . . . and the sky . . . and mountains . . . mountains everywhere you look. Nothing else.

Nothing else in your head.

WIDOW. So it's not like looking at them out of a plane window?

GRIZZLY. Not really.

So I'd miss that. A lot.

But this is brilliant, you know, this is just . . .

The WIDOW *snuggles into him.*

WIDOW. Yeah, definitely worth risking the job for . . .

GNOME stirs, they both look over.

Come on, you need to get up. We can't, not in here.

GRIZZLY. I know. I just wanted . . . There's not a lot of intimacy in a drugs cupboard. But it's fucking hot.

WIDOW. Yeah.

GRIZZLY. Isn't it though?

They kiss.

WIDOW. I'll lose my job. I need to clock in in five anyway.

GRIZZLY lets her go. They sit up, straightening themselves out. They move away from GNOME's bedside.

GRIZZLY. How is she doing? Really?

WIDOW. No one's lying to you. She's stable. All her vital signs are strong. We just have to wait for her to wake up.

GRIZZLY. It's just I've been three weeks living off hospital food. Don't know how much more I can take.

WIDOW. They're doing everything they can.

GRIZZLY. Beats paying London prices for a B and B, of course, but still . . .

WIDOW. If you needed to go home for a while . . . I could ring you as soon as there was any change.

GRIZZLY. Oh, I'm no going anywhere.

See, what I mean is . .

I don't feel right being this happy. But I am. So. There you go. This was in my head anyway, and then you were like this big chance at the right time. Feels like it's all meant or something. And it's for the Gnome too, you see. It's like a deal, you know, a deal with . . . myself I suppose . . . or some bit of my head that just can't get past this great lump of rock and ice . . . Anyway . . . You don't need to know about that. That's mad.

What I need to ask you is . . .

He can't do it.

WIDOW (*troubled*). Colin . . . I don't think . . .

GRIZZLY. No, give me a chance. I can do this.

I do need to sort my life out, I know that so . . . What I need to ask is . . .

I suppose it's the million dollar question.

WIDOW. What?

GRIZZLY. Do you mind if I stick my ice axe in your hall cupboard?

Long pause.

WIDOW. Well . . . I don't know . . . Because I wasn't actually planning on taking you home.

Sorry.

I didn't realise you were . . .

Look . . . This is just a mad thing we do here. Just here. It's a bad time for you, I know what that's like. It was a very bad night for me when I met you and you held me together. So thank you. Thank you for being mad with me.

I'm not taking that home. Not into my house. Not in front of my kids. Do you understand?

GRIZZLY. Aye OK. (*Pause.*) No, I fucking don't. What have we been doing?

WIDOW. You've got a dead brother, I've got a dead husband. It's the bottom line for both of us. It's why we're not fit for anything except this.

GRIZZLY. All right. Let me tell you. When I look at you I am not thinking about death.

WIDOW. Then you're an idiot because that's all I've got.

I'm not going to lose the best part of my life by pretending anything could ever be that good again. So I had that, and now all I have is this.

GRIZZLY. What?

WIDOW. Guys . . . like you.

GRIZZLY. Right. You know what I think you need to do . . .

WIDOW. What? Get over it? Move on? Let the dead go? I don't see any need to do that, ever, do you?

GRIZZLY. I was just going to say, if that's true . . . you need to date men that can afford hotel rooms.

Or men who sleep in houses.

WIDOW. They're in the waiting area. Their heads are full of death. They can smell it. I look at them. I smile. It's that easy. I'm in death's waiting room but they can see my heartbeat. I've got a key to a locked door, where nothing will find us for five minutes, not death or anyone else they know. It's that simple. That's who I am, the daily special in death's waiting room.

GRIZZLY. Look, this wasny like that for me, I really . . .

WIDOW. I'm not talking about you! I'm talking about what I did five minutes before I met you. What I always do!

GRIZZLY. Oh . . . right.

Serious? You shagged some bloke just before you found me . . . ?

WIDOW. Yes!

GRIZZLY. Why would you do that?

WIDOW. I just told you.

GRIZZLY. Did you? I don't . . . I'm not getting this . . .

The WIDOW *turns away from him.*

But I suppose this is pretty fucking stupid of me, eh?

WIDOW. This time next month you'll be on a mountain with nothing in your head.

GRIZZLY (*grabbing her*). OK, OK, we're both fuck ups? That what you're saying? The bottom dropped out of the world and we both fell all the way down. One day, one moment, and we're ruined forever. Yes?

The night I met you . . . I decided. I'm not having it. I'm turning that on its head.

One moment, one choice and we're *fixed* forever because if it's that easy to fall I'll make it that easy to bounce. Fuck fate. Fuck tragedy! If I'm more than half way to the end then I'm going *up* for the rest of it. What do you say? You coming?

WIDOW. Jesus Christ. Who are you? Where's the collecting tin . . .

GRIZZLY (*interrupting*). One moment. Just change! Do it!

The WIDOW *hesitates. She hangs on the edge.*

WIDOW. I woke up first . . . I always do . . . He never hears the alarm . . . He never heard the alarm . . .

GRIZZLY. Darlin' . . .

WIDOW (*pitching over him*). And I brought him a coffee, I always did that if I wasn't on a late shift . . . and he seemed in good spirits. He seemed like his usual self, he made the joke he always made that I was his morning geisha, waiting on him hand and foot. He always did that, it always annoyed me . . . but we laughed. We always laughed.

GRIZZLY. I know you can't ever . . .

WIDOW (*cutting over again*). This was our morning routine! It was all just as it usually was. This was our life.

I heard him whistling when he was shaving. He shouted through the door that the Billy's toothbrush was dry and Billy had to get back in and do his teeth properly . . .

He was just the way he always was . . .

I know it was a big day for him. I know there was a lot hanging on it. But . . . that's the way it is when you're running your own business, isn't it? It's so up and down . . . We always pulled through . . . And if this time he hadn't . . . if he'd lost everything . . . we would still have managed . . . we were a team.

He said goodbye to Billy, he kissed the baby . . . He said goodbye to me . . . There was nothing . . . nothing on his face, nothing that made me think he was stressed or upset or . . .

I always watched him leave out the window. I waved. He waved. He smiled.

The bus driver thought Dave was looking at the bus when he stepped out . .

Why would he do that? Maybe he was looking and he didn't see. If he was thinking hard, if he was worrying . . .

How could he do that? How could he throw away our whole life? It had to be an accident.

DOG *enters under this. They don't see him.*

How can an accident like that happen? How can everything you feel, all your . . . *love*, be made so small in one second?

I'll never be that small, Colin Ross. I'll never let everything I am, all my love shrivel into that limp and wrinkled and empty thing called '*getting over it*'. Do you understand!?

GRIZZLY. Pete's still up there.

WIDOW. What?

GRIZZLY. Dog saw him. Sitting there. Just where I left him. Pete's still up there.

But I'm not going back for him!

Pause.

WIDOW. Well, why the hell not? If I could touch his face one more time, I'd climb a fucking mountain to do it.

GRIZZLY *turns from her abruptly and goes back to* GNOME.

The WIDOW *sees* DOG *watching her.*

WIDOW. Something you want here?

DOG. No . . . thanks.

WIDOW. No. Well, get off the ward, visiting hours are over.

DOG *watches her leave then exits himself.*

GRIZZLY *leans over* GNOME, *she stirs, her face turns towards him. She wakes up.*

GNOME. When are we going up the hill, Dad?

GRIZZLY. Anytime you like, pet.

GRIZZLY *stands looking up the mountain as the wind rises. Mixed into it is a sound like laboured breathing.*

The light fades.

ACT TWO

A Cliff Face

Three months later.

GRIZZLY and DOG appear, they're on a day climb, acclimatisation. Ice face.

DOG is leading, GRIZZLY waits below, hanging off his ropes, relaxed, feeling the sun on his face. They're close enough to talk comfortably.

DOG is just completing a difficult stretch. He places the ice screw and rests, tied off on it, leaning out to look at the sky like GRIZZLY.

GRIZZLY is having a smoke.

DOG (*the sky*). What colour would you call that?

GRIZZLY. Navy blue.

DOG. Cobalt.

GRIZZLY. Cobalt?

DOG. Yeah.

GRIZZLY. You'd call that cobalt?

DOG. I would.

GRIZZLY. That's very descriptive.

DOG. You think?

GRIZZLY. Very artistic.

DOG. Yeah.

GRIZZLY. Is that like an interior design thing? You read that off a Dulux colour chart? You going to paint your kitchenette cobalt?

DOG. Might do.

GRIZZLY. I thought cobalt was a stone?

DOG. You get the colour from the stone.

GRIZZLY. You've been on the pub quiz machine, haven't you?

DOG is eyeing up the next stretch, he's psyching himself up for a difficult manoeuvre, jumping a section over a sheer drop.

DOG. I'll need some rope in a minute.

GRIZZLY (*seeing what he's planning*). Give it up, man, it'll kill you.

DOG. Money on? Come on, money on?

GRIZZLY. It's suicide, man, give it up.

DOG. You think it's suicide? You think I'm going to die here?

GRIZZLY. Yeah!

DOG. Bet you I don't.

GRIZZLY. I bet you fucking do.

DOG. I'll take that bet. Can't lose. Can't pay up if I lose.

GRIZZLY. Aw, Dog man.

DOG. What?

GRIZZLY. You're making me tired.

DOG. Everything's making you tired, Grizzle darling.

GRIZZLY. What?

DOG. Do you know what today is?

GRIZZLY. No?

DOG. It's our anniversary.

GRIZZLY. Is it?

DOG. Thirteen years.

GRIZZLY. Is it!?

DOG. Thirteen years ago today. I know because it's my Mum's birthday.

GRIZZLY. Happy birthday to the Dog Mum.

DOG. You calling my mum a bitch?

GRIZZLY. You got a problem with that?

DOG. No. Harsh but fair.

GRIZZLY. Fuck me. Thirteen years?

DOG. Yeah.

GRIZZLY. Jesus, that means it's nine since we did Gualong?

DOG. Ten years next May.

GRIZZLY. Fuck. Never knew it was that long. I need to stop talking about it the way I do. 'Oh yes, Dog and me did the first ascent of Gualong,' it's history, isn't it? I'll look like a twat.

DOG. Strange how often that happens.

GRIZZLY. Just trying to make you feel a little less alone.

Pause.

DOG. How long did you and Pete climb together?

GRIZZLY. Well, he got a start before I did . . .

DOG. Yeah, but how many years did you do together?

GRIZZLY. Must have been . . . I wasn't long past eighteen. (*Calculating.*) Must have been twelve years.

DOG. Thought so, thought we'd done one more. (*Looking up.*) I do love that colour. Half way to outer space.

Thin air.

Thin, thin air.

GRIZZLY. Not often I complain but wind chill is setting in.

DOG. Oh, we're all in a hurry.

We are going to hammer that bastard mountain this year.

GRIZZLY. Fuck's sake . . .

DOG. What?

Oh fuck, sorry. Tempting fate. Excuse me. No one's listening, you know. When did you get so superstitious?

GRIZZLY. I'm not superstitious.

DOG. You fucking are these days.

GRIZZLY. If my Dad's Dad was on his way to work and he saw a woman, he'd turn round and go home. Lose a day's pay. *That's* superstitious.

DOG. Well, that's common sense. He knew trouble when he saw it.

GRIZZLY *doesn't reply.*

None of my business.

GRIZZLY. What isn't?

DOG. Nothing. I'm not going to say it.

Pause.

I never thought she was a good idea.

GRIZZLY. Who?

DOG. The Angel of fucking death.

Pause.

You're not going to see her again, are you?

GRIZZLY. Not unless I'm flat on my face with a tube up my arse.

DOG. I knew you were kinky.

GRIZZLY. She was grieving, man. It wasn't her fault.

DOG. If you say so.

So do you reckon she'd kept her monkey locked up since he went?

GRIZZLY. Shut up, Dog.

DOG. No, it's just I can't imagine anyone doing that for me.

GRIZZLY. No, I can imagine you'd put a woman off sex for years.

DOG. I'm a hard act to follow, I'll give you that.

GRIZZLY. Last time you were hard you were watching your sister undress.

DOG. Didn't hear your mum complaining.

GRIZZLY. No, that was a pity fuck, mate.

DOG. She wanted it, and she was prepared to pay.

Did you hear about that woman in Italy?

GRIZZLY. What woman in Italy?

DOG. Her bloke dies half way down the Andes . . . in the Cordillera Blanca I think it was . . . And she's sure he's still up there. So she's got all her life savings and she's funding this expedition to go and find him. Fucking thousands of dollars, not to climb the thing, just to bring him back.

I just wouldn't go near a gig like that. Would you?

Rope please.

GRIZZLY *gives him a little more rope.*

The thing is. That is not going to end well for her, is it?

They're not going to find him holed up in a snow cave having a beer with the Abominable Snow Man, are they? (*Looking at watch.*) 'Oh shit is that the time?' *Rope,* Grizzly!

Reluctantly GRIZZLY *gives him a little more.*

So how bad would it be . . . how bad would it be if they find he pegged out shagging a llama? How'd you break it to her?

Still nothing.

Well . . . He died happy . . . and quite warm . . .

GRIZZLY. Maybe she just needs to know she's tried as hard as she could. Maybe she just needs to know she gave him that when she remembers him. Maybe he was a big enough part of her she needs to do that . . .

DOG goes for the leap, he stacks it and vanishes from sight.

GRIZZLY *holds him. Just.*

Silence, GRIZZLY *straining, then the sound of* DOG *laughing hysterically below.*

GRIZZLY *makes the rope safe.* DOG *appears below, jumaring up it. He has blood on him, helmet knocked squint. He's still laughing.*

At the same time we see the mountain start to grow again above them. GNOME *is in full kit, setting up a camp. Effort, carrying kit at altitude, working hard.*

DOG. All right . . . how much do I owe you?

GRIZZLY. I didn't take the bet, Dog.

DOG. Didn't win the bet, still here, aren't I? Still here. On our way. Four months from now we'll be back there, Grizzly. Man, that is a big climb. A big, fucking climb. We're going to be ready. Fit and ready. Sun on our faces, Gnome at our backs getting a brew ready . . . if she's fit by then.

GRIZZLY. She'll be fit.

DOG. Then we're on our way.

DOG is back on the ledge beside GRIZZLY.

So glad we're going for that climb again, man. When you said you were giving up . . .

GRIZZLY. Got to stop sometime . . .

DOG. You can stop when you fall off. I knew we'd be doing this. I knew we'd be back training up for the big one.

GRIZZLY. Yes. (*Checking out* DOG's *injury.*) Need to get something on that, Dog.

DOG. Yeah, yeah, sort it out at the bottom. Quicker going up to go down now anyway.

DOG *indicates the face he's just fallen off.*

Your lead.

GRIZZLY (*sorting out ropes*). Thought it might be.

GRIZZLY *starts to climb, a different line to* DOG.

DOG. Aw fuck, man, that is such a chicken run.

GRIZZLY. Dog, some days you've just got to go the easy way.

GRIZZLY *is concentrating on his work.*

DOG. Grizzly? Tell me we're not just going back because Pete's there. Tell me we're going to climb the hill, Grizzle.

GRIZZLY. We always climb the hill, Dog, that's what we do.

GRIZZLY *climbs up.*

On the Mountain

Four months later. High camp on the mountain. 6,500 metres to the summit.

Like a time-lapsed film we see the sunlight move over it. Again we hear the roar, the distant sound of storms, avalanches, a steady rumble as if the mountain itself was growling with menace.

GRIZZLY *climbs up to the ledge where* GNOME *has set up the camp. They are all much more tired, days of climbing behind him. The air is thinner but they're acclimatised. They can talk fairly easily.*

DOG *is close behind* GRIZZLY.

DOG (*looking round the ledge*). God, it's a palace.

GNOME. I know. We don't even have to draw lots for whose arse is hanging out in space.

DOG. I wish we'd found this last time.

GNOME. Someone did. There's an old pin in that crack down there, did you see?

GRIZZLY. I think that was me and Pete.

There's an awkward silence for a minute, then a distant roar, higher up the mountain.

Fuck.

The snow train to oblivion.

DOG. Half the fucking hill came off then, didn't it?

GRIZZLY. Wait a bit.

DOG. What are we looking for?

GRIZZLY. The sparkle.

DOG. What are you on about now?

GRIZZLY. Takes a few minutes after an avalanche then you can see it. All the ice crystals thrown up in the air. Look!

DOG. Fuck yeah, it's like that . . . what is it? Out of Peter Pan.

GRIZZLY. Sparkle.

DOG. Pixie dust.

Pause.

GRIZZLY. Did you just say pixie dust?

DOG. No.

GRIZZLY. You did.

DOG. I'm not saying that, you can't make me say that.

DOG *is still looking up the mountain.*

Hey Grizzle, look at this.

GRIZZLY (*working*). What?

DOG. Come and see.

GRIZZLY *comes to join him, looking up the mountain.*

I think we can do it in a oner. Look, if we take that line there, look . . . See what I mean? Bit of hard slog to start but then we can swing over that traverse and then we're nearly at the base of the rock band. Piece of cake. What do you think?

GRIZZLY *says nothing for a moment.*

We'd have knocked it off this time tomorrow.

GRIZZLY *still says nothing.*

Or we could bivvy at the base of the rock band . . . if you think the Gnome couldn't do the pace?

GRIZZLY. That's not the right line, man.

DOG. Yeah, come on, just look a second if we start up towards those seracs and . . .

GRIZZLY. No, that's not the way we went.

DOG. Who?

GRIZZLY. Me and Pete.

DOG *says nothing.*

Look, if the weather had been right, me and Pete would have made it from there. If the weather's right tomorrow you and me will make it from there.

DOG. Great.

GRIZZLY. You sure?

DOG (*really, really angry, not showing it*). Yeah. No problem.

DOG *turns away and starts working on the camp, vanishing into the tent.* GRIZZLY *looks back up the mountain for a moment then he turns to work too, chipping out ice for water.*

GNOME *waits for a last look at the sky, watching it darken, the moon come up. After a moment* GRIZZLY *comes out of the tent. He moves out of* GNOME*'s eyeline, turning away, trying to take a piss off the ledge.*

GRIZZLY (*nothing much is happening*). Fuck.

GNOME. I know. I couldn't either.

GRIZZLY. Ach well. Got something out. The Dog's not even trying. That is why he's called the Dog, if you're wondering, fifty below and he still won't use a bottle. Got to find a tree.

GNOME. Not many round here.

GNOME *still looks up at the sky and the mountain.*

It is a perfect night. No wind. Give it a chance to freeze and you can head up in great style.

GRIZZLY. Are you not coming, honey?

GNOME. Nah. Doesn't feel right.

GRIZZLY. You've done brilliantly.

GNOME. I'm happy but I'm still not a hundred percent. I can feel it.

GRIZZLY. You sure?

GNOME. Sure. I'm stopping here.

GRIZZLY *suddenly slumps, physically sagging with relief.*

GRIZZLY. Good. That's good, Gnomey.

You're stopping here. You're stopping here. That's great.

GNOME. Yeah?

GRIZZLY. Fixed ropes down to base – you could skip down, darling. You'll be all right.

GNOME. I was always going to be all right, Grizzly.

GRIZZLY. I know, pet, just . . . being back here . . .

GNOME. I'll have a brew ready for you coming back.

GRIZZLY. I should never have let you come.

GNOME. I was up for it.

GRIZZLY. I know.

GNOME. I knew I was fit to come and now I know I should stop. *I* know what I'm doing, Grizzly.

GRIZZLY. Course you do. This is me, Gnomey. This is just me. (*Pause.*) Come on then, you'll freeze your tits off out here.

GNOME. There's five minutes heat left in that sun and I'm having all of it. (*Pointing.*) The moon's coming up.

They watch the view in silence for a moment. They move close together and hold onto each other for warmth.

I like the moon.

GRIZZLY. Do you, pet?

GNOME. You know what I think? I think if the moon was a person it'd like me.

GRIZZLY. Oh aye, why's that?

GNOME. Because I'd leave it alone.

Pause.

GRIZZLY. You don't do drugs, do you, Gnomey?

GNOME. No.

GRIZZLY. No explanation then.

GNOME. That's where I was actually, when I was out of it, I was on the moon.

GRIZZLY. Were you?

GNOME. It was the land of the dead. They were all sitting round on moon rocks, pretty miserable, wishing they were alive again. But they were quite nice to me. Very friendly in a depressed sort of way. And the Moon told me I was quite welcome to stay as long as I liked but not to go leaping about or bouldering or anything.

GRIZZLY. Well, I hope you didn't.

GNOME. Oh no, I was very well behaved. I just waited, with everyone else.

I think I played chess with this dead, old black guy . . .

GRIZZLY. No, that was after you woke up.

GNOME. Was it? I thought that was on the moon.

'Course I was on drugs then . . .

GRIZZLY. You were. They were fantastic. We were so jealous but you wouldn't share.

GNOME. It's just great to be up here.

Pause.

GRIZZLY. You know, when I was very wee, I thought I was going to climb the mountains on the moon one day.

GNOME. Did you?

GRIZZLY. Yeah, I thought we were all going to be living up there with Neil Armstrong and James Burke.

GNOME. Who?

GRIZZLY. Stop being so fucking young.

GNOME (*looking up the mountain*). Aw, wow!

*A distant rumble. They watch the avalanche far away,
higher up the slope.*

I don't like a mountain that gives you avalanches after dark.

GRIZZLY. No.

GNOME. Dog really wants this one, doesn't he?

GRIZZLY. Dog really wants every climb.

GNOME. Thing is, you do climb with other people.

GRIZZLY. Yeah . . . muck about now and then with the old
gang but so does Dog . . .

GNOME. No. He doesn't. Only when you're there too.

GRIZZLY. It's a body odour thing. I have told him. He climbs
with you.

GNOME. You climb with me. And Dog doesn't mind me being
here.

GRIZZLY. Well, you're no bother.

GNOME. That's the one.

I wouldn't climb with him without you, Grizzly. No one
would.

GRIZZLY. Aw, come on . . .

GNOME. He tells you what he thinks about the line you're
taking up a bit of rock while you're climbing . . . *while
you're climbing*, Grizzly. 'Fuck's sake, Gnome, there's a
hold right by your ear.'

GRIZZLY (*laughing*). Yeah, yeah you're right. No one but me
would stand for it.

GNOME. I love you guys. Love you. You were my heroes, you
know. Read about every climb you ever made. You inspired
me.

GRIZZLY. That's fucking sad, Gnome.

GNOME. Isn't it though?

You're beautiful to watch. I just want to save you.

Looking up at mountain.

Got to know when to stop, haven't you?

55

GRIZZLY. Are you superstitious, Gnomey?

GNOME. No.

GRIZZLY. So if you'd made a deal . . . and you'd skipped out of paying it, what do you think would happen?

GNOME. Who have I made the deal with?

GRIZZLY. The Universe.

GNOME. Oh the *Universe*. No ducking out of that one. It'll make you pay up one way or another.

GRIZZLY. That's what I reckoned.

GNOME (*looking at the sunset*). Last bit of warmth. The freezer door's shutting on us any second.

GRIZZLY. Pete's up there, Gnomey.

GNOME. I know.

What was the sky like that night? The night before you went up last time?

GRIZZLY. Just like this.

GNOME. Need to keep an eye out then. The sky could lie to you again.

GRIZZLY. Yes.

We headed up about four. Pete was in great form. Going like a train . . . I wasn't doing so well, putting all my energy into breathing but he was going great guns . . . One bit I was leading and he was waiting behind me . . . He was moving as much as he could, you know . . . keeping warm . . . And what he always did was whistle through his teeth . . . which is bad luck of course . . . bring the wind . . . but he didn't care . . . and I could hear him trying to whistle . . . just like usual . . . but he didn't have the breath . . . and I heard him laugh about it . . . He was in great form . . .

GNOME. How high did you get?

GRIZZLY. I don't actually remember. We must have been close when we turned back. Pete was leading . . . I'd slowed right down . . . my chest wasn't good that day . . . he'd led the last three pitches and I'd just been trying to keep up . . . and I saw this massive front building up over to the east . . . At the time it seemed like it came out of nowhere . . . but . . . you know . . . I don't think we'd been looking . . . it was . . .

you know what it's like. No oxygen, your heads full of porridge . . .

GNOME. Can't think . . .

GRIZZLY. No. I wasn't thinking at all. If Pete had gone on up I'd just have followed. But he didn't. He said we should go down. I know we were very close to the top then but he was very clear, very sure, he was absolutely in control at that point, he knew it was too dangerous for us to stay up there. So we turned back.

And the storm hit when we were on the way down . . . I could barely see him on the way down . . . just the rope tight then slack between us . . . The first idea I had there was anything wrong was when I got to this broader ledge . . .

GNOME. Here?

GRIZZLY. Higher up. We were aiming for this ledge. We never made it.

The wind chill was straight out of hell, Gnomey. Storm in my eyes. In my throat. It was dark . . . it was wild . . . and I'm thinking when Pete gets down we should bivvy where we are because it was too rough to keep going . . . but he doesn't show and he doesn't show . . . So I'm trying to get the bivvy tent out and get it up . . . and I've nearly done it by the time he finally shows . . . and it's when I'm shouting I think we need to stay here till the storm clears . . . and I can see he's not hearing me . . . he's sort of . . . groggy . . . But I just thought . . . well, we were both done in . . .

GNOME. Yes.

GRIZZLY. Even for the first part of the night . . . I thought he was fine . . . He was talking to me . . . He was a bit out of it . . . but, you know, so was I . . . but he kept saying he had a headache . . . and then he stopped making sense . . . he was rambling . . . I said 'You're doing fine, Pete.' He said 'Stop tugging me,' I kept telling him he was doing fine, he kept saying 'Stop tugging me, stop pulling on me, I'm no going in there, I'm no going in the fucking dark . . . ' I wasn't touching him.

I thought, you know, he was talking about the pit. He hated going down the pit . . .

And finally I did think, 'Oh fuck, cerebral odema' . . . But I didn't know what to do . . . I didn't know what I could do

57

except pray the storm blew itself out so I could get him lower down . . .

And he didn't seem so bad after a while. And then he said, clear as anything, 'Col, are you there?' And I said, 'I'm here.' And he said, 'Don't leave me, will you?' And that was the last thing he said.

Pause.

GNOME. Sun's gone, Grizzly. We need to get in.

GRIZZLY. Yeah.

GNOME. You're going for it tomorrow?

GRIZZLY. Sky looks OK. We're going for it tomorrow. (*Rallying.*) Where's my fucking tea? Thought you were getting a brew on?

GNOME. All right, Dad.

GNOME goes to the tent. GRIZZLY is still staring up the hill. Just for a moment there seems to be a figure above him, hanging off ropes, looking down at him. GRIZZLY looks, then goes into the tent.

Lighting change. Darkness falls over the mountain. Two head torches go on in the tent. The men getting ready for the climb. It's about 4.00 a.m.

After a moment, first DOG, then GRIZZLY crawl out of the tent and start the climb up. As they climb the tent vanishes below.

They have been climbing for hours, the camp is now a long way below them.

The dawn is coming up on the mountain. It reveals the body of a climber, slumped on a narrow ledge just above DOG.

DOG has reached the ledge. He sees the dead climber. He looks at him for a long moment. He ties off. He tugs on the rope, signalling below.

GRIZZLY reaches the ledge.

He too stands for a long moment, looking at the dead climber.

He ties off. At this height both he and DOG are much more breathless. Conversation is more laboured.

Slowly, GRIZZLY edges over and leans over the dead climber.

58

DOG. Are you . . . all right, Grizzly?

GRIZZLY *doesn't answer for a long moment.*

What do you . . . want to do, mate?

GRIZZLY. I don't think . . . it's him.

GRIZZLY *is looking around the body.*

There ought to be . . . a bit of the bivvy tent . . . left or . . . something.

He hesitates for a long moment, then very gently and awkwardly he starts to look in the dead man's pockets. He peels his outer glove off with his teeth and tugs gingerly at the frozen zips.

He takes out a small bundle. He looks at it.

It's not him.

DOG. Must be the Japanese guy.

GRIZZLY. Must be the Japanese guy.

GRIZZLY *slumps on the ledge beside the dead climber.*

DOG *waits.*

DOG. You OK?

GRIZZLY. Aye.

DOG. You're sure.

GRIZZLY. Yeah, yeah . . . I'm OK, man . . . thanks? We should . . .

He's frozen into the rock, Dog. We should let him go, but . . .

DOG. Take us hours. He's part of the ice now. Poor fucker.

GRIZZLY *still doesn't move.* DOG *tries to maintain respectful stillness but he starts to fidget.*

He looks up, scanning the route above.

So what . . . do you want . . . to do?

GRIZZLY *doesn't answer.*

DOG *leans back, looking at the route.*

God . . . you were close. You were . . . so close.

Still nothing.

We can do it.

GRIZZLY *looks then, looking at the route. Looking at the sky.*

We're . . . going . . . to do it.

GRIZZLY *is studying the sky.*

What . . . do you reckon?

Nothing.

I think . . . go for it . . . Not for me to say but . . .

Fuck man . . . let's . . . go for it.

GRIZZLY (*pointing*). Front . . . need to go down.

DOG. No . . .

GRIZZLY. Front . . . coming . . . no time . . .

DOG. There's . . . time.

GRIZZLY. No.

DOG *hates this. He waits, just looking at* GRIZZLY.

Got . . . to . . . go down.

DOG. I . . . think . . . we could make it.

GRIZZLY. No.

DOG. But . . . I think . . .

GRIZZLY. *No!* . . . Come on . . . going down . . .

A stand off, there's nothing DOG *can do.*

DOG. All right . . . if . . . you want.

GRIZZLY. We're going down.

They still wait.

You . . . first.

DOG *hesitates again, then starts down the ropes.*

GRIZZLY *looks at the dead climber for a long time, then he follows.*

The front moving over the mountain, a growing shadow as they vanish below, a growing whistling hum, the approaching storm, for a moment the sound of laboured breathing seems to be mixed into it.

Lights down on the mountain as darkness falls. Slowly coming up on the tent. This time we can see inside.

DOG *and* GRIZZLY *are sitting crushed in with* GNOME, *they are rubbing feet and hands, trying to get their circulation going.* GNOME *helping them.*

The wind suddenly hits like a hammer. The noise is incredible, the canvas of the tent flapping madly. It's rapidly getting completely dark.

GRIZZLY, DOG *and* GNOME *keep rubbing and rubbing as the storm rages outside.*

The frail lamplight in the tent is a little bubble of warmth suspended against the side of the dark, roaring mountain.

Lighting change. Hours pass.

Night. They are trapped in the tent. The storm buffeting them. The wind is no longer deafening but snow flies past horizontally as the wind buffets the tent.

They're sitting very close together, heaped on top of each other, sharing each other's heat.

DOG *makes a sound of satisfaction.*

DOG. Moved my toes.

GRIZZLY. That's good.

DOG. I know.

> DOG *gets out cigarettes, gives one to* GRIZZLY, *offers the* GNOME. GNOME *shakes her head.*

GRIZZLY. Good time to start.

DOG. How many have we got left?

GRIZZLY. Last packet.

DOG. Crap time for her to start then. Shut up, Grizzly.

Pause.

GNOME. Worst screen death.

DOG. Define worst.

GNOME. Biggest tear-jerker. Made you cry.

DOG (*groaning*). You see I can't do that one. I was thinking that head vice thing in *Casino* or . . .

GRIZZLY. The Dog has no tears.

GNOME. Bambi's Mum.

They all groan in unison.

GRIZZLY. That's bad.

DOG. No.

GRIZZLY. Dog, you can't tell us you didn't cry when Bambi's Mum ate lead.

DOG. I ate Bambi's Mum.

GRIZZLY. You're not human.

DOG. Venison burgers. Yum.

GRIZZLY. *E.T.*

GNOME. I cried at that.

DOG. E.T's not dead.

GRIZZLY. When you think he is.

DOG. I never thought he was. He was a hunk of latex.

GRIZZLY. So when you look in the mirror, Dog, do you have a reflection? Darth Vador.

GNOME. No, that was pants.

DOG. Awful.

GNOME. Ruler of the dark side . . . Helmet off . . . wrinkly and cuddly. Wrong.

DOG. You cried at that?

GRIZZLY. I might have done.

DOG. What the *fuck?*

GRIZZLY. He was Luke's Dad! He wanted to see him with his own eyes before he died!

GNOME. I don't know anyone who thought that was a good film.

DOG. Grizzly probably fancied the Ewoks.

GRIZZLY. You're the expert on animal passion, Dog.

DOG. I'm not the one with fur.

GRIZZLY. What was your last girlfriend called?

Sheep noise.

Baaaaarbara, wasn't it?

DOG. Nothing really dies in kids' films.

GNOME (*agreeing*). *Jungle Book*. Baloo.

DOG. That runty little dalmatian.

GRIZZLY (*contradiction*). Simba's Dad . . .

All chorus together.

ALL. Bambi's Mum.

DOG. Yeah, Bambi's Mum is bad.

GRIZZLY. You did cry, didn't you, Dog?

DOG. It's good though, it is good, things die. Kids should know that.

GRIZZLY. Little puppy tears rolling down your muzzle . . .

DOG. Yeah, yeah . . .

GRIZZLY. Kids shouldn't know things die. No one should. It robs you of faith in the future. Kids should think we're immortal.

GNOME. Kids do think they're immortal.

DOG. Things die, grow up, get over it.

Awkward pause.

GNOME. Me then? OK . . . Best love story.

DOG. I don't do chick flicks.

GNOME. I can't think of another one. You do one, Grizzly.

GRIZZLY. Right eh . . .

DOG. Come on, man. Keep it going.

GRIZZLY. I'm thinking, I'm thinking . . .

DOG *looks at watch.*

What?

DOG *says nothing.*

What?

DOG. Nothing.

GRIZZLY. You think we would have made it?

DOG. It doesn't matter.

GRIZZLY. You think we had enough time. You think we would have made it? Is that what you're saying?

DOG. Yes, I think we would have made it! But it doesn't matter, all right!

Just leave it.

GRIZZLY. We were two hours from the summit. At least.

DOG. All right.

GRIZZLY. At least two hours.

DOG. Which means we would have made it! It's all right, man . . . I'm just . . . disappointed . . . Let's just drop it, OK? Not your fault.

GRIZZLY. Not my *fault*?

DOG. Just drop it!

GRIZZLY. Not my fault that I got you in out of the hell that's going on out there?

DOG. I think we could have made it up and back in time. Yes. But, it's OK.

GRIZZLY. Fucking right it's OK.

GNOME. Guys . . .

GRIZZLY. Fucking right it is! I called it right. I saw the storm coming. The storm is here.

DOG. Whatever.

GRIZZLY. Well, isn't it?

DOG. Yes, Grizzly. It is. Well done. My fucking saviour. Now shut up, will you?

GRIZZLY. You can't beat the odds for ever, Dog.

DOG. Oh, I don't believe this! Are we going with the old man of the mountains routine then?

GRIZZLY. Give me a fucking break.

DOG. All right, gramps . . .

GRIZZLY (*meaning it*). Fuck off, Dog.

GNOME (*quietly*). The wind's dropping.

DOG. Grizzly . . . We were going strong. We were going great. You wanted to come down. What do you want me to say?

GRIZZLY. It was a judgement call and I was ri . . .

DOG. I don't know when we'll get back here. Do you? You're messing me around, Grizzly, you're messing me up . . . I did two fucking horrible dead end jobs, seven days a week for seven months to get here last time and I did it again to get here this time and I'm just not looking forward to doing it again with nothing to show for it, that's all.

GRIZZLY. Oh, is this about money? You want me to pay your expenses, Dog.

DOG. Oh yeah, that's right. You pay. With what? Your lottery number coming up?

GRIZZLY. You want it now? I'll fucking give it to you now . . .

DOG. You got the money now?

GRIZZLY. First second we get down . . .

DOG. Oh, when we get down. What'll you do then? Get out your cash card? You got any money in the bank, Grizzly?

GRIZZLY. You'll get your fucking money.

DOG. What'll you do? Sell your flat? Oh shit, can't can you, you're in rented, aren't you, mate? Never mind, sell your car maybe, pawn off the family heirlooms? No? Bit strapped for assets, aren't you, mate? So what have you got? Do you remember?

GRIZZLY. All right, Dog . . .

DOG. You've got the same as me! The same as me, Grizzly, difference is I don't give a fuck! I'm still glad I've got a life!

GNOME. Stop this. Stop this.

DOG. You need to remember why you're here at all.

GRIZZLY *says nothing.*

GNOME. Dog. Stop.

DOG. I don't know what's up. Ever since Gnomey was in the hospital you've been away somewhere and I don't even have a map to get there!

GRIZZLY. Dog, you just don't want to believe I'm jacking it in.

DOG. All right, I believe you. So why are you here?

GRIZZLY *says nothing.*

You'll go up the hill for him but not for me. Is that how it goes?

Still nothing.

You'll go up the hill for a dead man but not me, is that it?

Nothing.

We've hardly done a decent climb you hadn't done with him first. My whole career has been a memorial to a corpse I never even knew!

GRIZZLY. Career?! You think this is a . . .

DOG (*cutting over him*). Thirteen fucking years! Count them!

DOG *is taken with a coughing fit, shaking them all. Finally it dies down.*

GNOME (*quietly and bitterly, to herself*). This is not fun. I am not having fun. At all.

Pause.

DOG. So. He's not here after all. So we're going home.

GRIZZLY. That's not it.

DOG. What is it then?

GRIZZLY. I said I would quit! I promised I would quit if she was OK.

Well, she's fine. But here I am. So what happens now!?

They're just looking at him.

Someone's going to get it, Dog. Someone's going to! And if it's not Gnomey it might be you and how do I live with that?!

DOG. You serious?

GRIZZLY. Yes!

DOG. So why did you come?

Pause.

GRIZZLY. I thought Pete was still here.

Pause.

DOG. So I'm right.

GRIZZLY. No. (*Pause.*) Yes.

Suddenly DOG *starts whacking at him, weak and breathless.* GNOME *quickly blocks him.*

GNOME. Fucking stop it! I am not kidding! I will throw you both down the hill! I will!

DOG *subsides, coughing.*

All right . . . I know I don't have the experience you guys do . . . I know I haven't done a third of the climbs . . . But from all I know . . . all I've heard . . . no one . . . I mean . . . no one . . . no matter how badly they want to kill the other guy . . . ever . . . ever . . . picks a fight above six thousand metres . . . there isn't enough fucking *air* for this shit!

There's silence but for the wind for a moment.

DOG. That woman did your head in. She was the angel of death and she filled your head with shit and it's still sitting in there. I can't stand it, Col.

Pause. GRIZZLY *says nothing.*

I fucked her, Grizzly. I fucked her when you were lying in the road. She took me in the drugs cupboard. That's it.

Pause.

GRIZZLY. Yeah, that's what I figured.

DOG. Nothing bad is going to happen to anyone. We're going for the top, tomorrow. Then you can tell me it's your last climb.

A pause, then GRIZZLY *stirs.*

GRIZZLY. Going for a dump.

GNOME (*quietly*). Careful, Grizzly, it's dark out there. The wind's still fierce.

GRIZZLY *leaves the tent.*

DOG. Do you think . . . ?

I shouldn't have told him.

GNOME *says nothing.*

It's just . . . All this crap about luck and death. I thought it would knock it on the head. He didn't shag death. *I* shagged death.

GNOME. I don't think it matters if you shag death. It's when you fall in love with it you've got problems.

GRIZZLY *goes to take a dump. There seems to be a*
shadowy figure climbing past him. He's crouching, looking
up at the shadowy climber. The wind gusts fiercely.
GRIZZLY *topples into his shit. He swears, trying to sort*
himself out. It's too cold, he's too exposed. He crawls back
to the tent.

DOG. Jesus!

GNOME *and* DOG *both react to the smell.*

What the fuck did you do? Sit in it?

GRIZZLY. Sorry.

DOG. Stick your fucking arse out the tent, freeze it off.

GRIZZLY (*shuffling out of the tent again*). Sorry.

GNOME. Grizzly? It's too cold. Come in.

DOG. Grizzly, get back here, you wanker.

GRIZZLY *is shuffling out of the tent, arse first.*

GRIZZLY. No . . . sorry . . . it's no right.

DOG *has started to laugh.* GNOME *joins in. They are both*
helpless, laughing and coughing.

DOG. Get in!

GNOME. Please get in, you're going to kill us.

DOG. Come on, man, your arse'll drop off.

GRIZZLY *clambers in.*

GNOME. Aw fuck, the smell'll kill us!

Still laughing, DOG *leans out quickly to close the tent.*

Just visible at the edge of the ledge, the figure of the climber
seems to be standing watching him.

DOG. Fuck!

GRIZZLY. You OK?

DOG. Yeah yeah . . .

He gets the tent closed. They start the ritual of rubbing
again, huddling close.

GNOME. You're costing me moisture, Grizzly, my eyes are
watering.

GRIZZLY. Think it's clearing.

If it passes over we could make a move for the top in a few hours.

What do you reckon, Dog?

DOG. Yeah . . . yeah . . . Let's go for it.

Lights down on the tent. The sound of the wind peaks and dies away.

It is very still.

Lights up on DOG *crouching over the stove, feeding the pan ice chips.*

GNOME *lies, an unmoving bundle in her sleeping bag.* GRIZZLY *is laboriously getting kitted up in the tiny space.* DOG *is nearly ready.*

He scrapes more ice and puts it in the pan. He tries to reach some of his gear. He knocks the pan over. He swears quietly.

GRIZZLY. Did you just knock the brew over?

DOG. Yes.

DOG starts scraping more ice to refill the pan.

GRIZZLY. That'll take hours. We don't have time.

Just drink what's there.

DOG offers the pan to GRIZZLY.

Take a fucking drink, man, don't be stupid.

DOG swigs at the pan then passes it to GRIZZLY. *His hands are shaking.* GRIZZLY *drinks as* DOG *packs up the other stove.*

DOG is wired, nervous, covering.

DOG reaches out and touches GRIZZLY*'s hand.*

DOG. Your hands are cold.

GRIZZLY. I'm fine.

They are both shuffling and wriggling into the last of their thick ice-climbing gear. GRIZZLY *leaves the tent to struggle into the last layers and ice boots. His fingers are slow and clumsy.* DOG *is little better.*

DOG. What's the sky like?

GRIZZLY. It's good.

DOG. Are you feeling all right?

GRIZZLY (*grins, meaning it*). Fantastic.

DOG. Fuck, I can't get going. We should get more fluid in us. This is fucking madness.

DOG laughs.

GRIZZLY. Yeah. Suicide probably. (*He gives a big grin.*) You ready?

DOG. The Gnome got enough gas?

GRIZZLY. Aye.

DOG. Lets get moving.

GNOME stirs as DOG forces his way out of the tent.

GNOME. Bye bye, Dog. Bye bye, Dad.

GRIZZLY. Don't go flying off to the moon now, and Gnomey? Don't wait up.

He zips the tent closed behind them.

GRIZZLY and DOG start to climb the sheer face above the ledge. DOG is leading. They climb up into darkness and vanish from sight.

GNOME (*quietly, almost to herself*). We're not tired. Not really. It just takes an hour to melt water to drink. Half an hour to take a shit. The air is thin and our feet are heavy. It's all right. It's slow. We're living above ourselves. We're fish trying to walk on top of the sea. It's all right. Go slow. Go careful and if you can't get up then slip back down again where it's thick and dark and warm. Time to go home. Time to go home.

My heart's running as fast as it can all the time, all the time, fluttering in my chest like a bird trapped in a locked room.

If you know where you're going you can get there. You can. I'm going home soon. I'm going home.

GNOME leaves the tent. She closes up the tent so we can no longer see in. She limps forward into the hospital.

Hospital

The WIDOW *is dressing and bandaging* GNOME's *frostbitten fingers.*

WIDOW. How did it happen?

GNOME. You don't need to do that.

WIDOW. I don't mind.

GNOME. They've been looked at.

WIDOW. No harm in looking again.

GNOME. It was an avalanche.

> *The* WIDOW *says nothing for a moment, concentrating on bandaging* GNOME's *hands.* GNOME *winces.*

WIDOW. Is that bit tender?

GNOME. Yes.

WIDOW. That's good, pain is good.

GNOME. I know.

> Did you really like him?

WIDOW. Who?

GNOME. Grizzly.

> *The* WIDOW *says nothing.*

> I think he really liked you.

WIDOW. We recognised each other.

GNOME. Is that what it was?

WIDOW. It was madness.

GNOME. Grizzly's a lot of things but he's not mad.

WIDOW. Depends how you look at it, doesn't it?

GNOME. Yeah. That's true. Depends where you are.

WIDOW. He was good. He was really good. But not for me.

GNOME. I never know what's good for me. I have to try
things to know that.

> *Pause.*

WIDOW. Did they get to the top?

GNOME. Yes.

I didn't hear the avalanche that took them off . . . I don't
think it went that far down the hill . . .

WIDOW. When did you know something had happened?

GNOME. By the middle of that night I was sure . . . the wind
dropped . . . And I heard this weird sound . . . It wasn't an
avalanche . . . It sounded like something flying low over the
tent . . . This strange . . . rushing sound . . . like a huge
bird . . . and I knew I had to go out . . . and look up the
hill . . . I thought . . . if they were trying to get down . . .
I could wave the torch . . . give them something to aim
for . . . (*She nearly loses it.*) I found the edge of the
avalanche, all the hill swept away. I tried digging, shouting
for them. I knew there was no chance but you just keep
trying things.

WIDOW. Yes. I know.

The WIDOW *has finished.* GNOME *gets up, putting part of
her climbing clothes back on.*

You'll be fine.

GNOME. Good.

Thanks.

Stupid. Lost a glove, digging for them.

They could have been anywhere. There was no chance really.

WIDOW. So why did you go?

GNOME. Because they might be alive. Luck's a funny thing eh?

I'm going back now. Aren't you coming?

WIDOW. No. I can't come now. I have to stay here.

The Mountain

GRIZZLY *and* DOG *appear, climbing up. They are only a few
feet below the summit, walking up.*

It's bright sunshine.

First GRIZZLY, *then* DOG, *reaches the top and stands, looking
out over all the other mountains. They have very little breath.*

GRIZZLY. That's . . . that done then.

They lean on their axes a moment. Moving slowly, they scrabble clumsily in pockets for cameras. GRIZZLY *photographs* DOG. DOG *photographs* GRIZZLY.

DOG. Anything . . . else . . . you want to do?

GRIZZLY *nods, groping in pockets again.*

GRIZZLY. That . . . guy . . . Japanese guy . . . his stuff.

He takes out the bundle he took off the dead climber, and slowly opens it out.

DOG. What . . . ?

GRIZZLY. Picture . . . 'nother mountain.

He lets it go onto the wind. He takes out something else. They both look.

DOG. What . . . is . . . it?

GRIZZLY. Dragon . . . Paper dragon.

He lets it go, and it flies off, trailing streamers.

DOG. Time to go . . . then . . .

GRIZZLY. Yeah . . . yeah . . . let's go . . .

They start to climb down.

Hours later. The light is fading. GRIZZLY *and* DOG *are now on the sheer face.* DOG *is waiting on a ledge.* GRIZZLY *is close above him. He's trying to clear the hill as he comes, pulling at a pin. It's hard work, and he's slowed right down.*

DOG. Leave it . . .

GRIZZLY *tries a moment longer but gives up. He descends to* DOG. *Gives one last impatient tug on the rope, then gives up. He unclips, ready to clip onto the rope* DOG *is on, to go further down. Just for a few moments, he's not tied on.*

His fingers are clumsy with cold, trying to clip on the next rope.

A rock falls from above, clattering down the face.

DOG. Jesus, Grizzly . . .

GRIZZLY (*intent on his fumbling fingers*). We're fine.

Another clatter of falling rocks. GRIZZLY *ducks against the face, shielding his head.*

The shadowy figure of a climber is higher up the hill looking down at them. DOG has seen it.

DOG. Grizzly!

GRIZZLY. It's only the edge . . . it's only the edge . . . it'll pass us by . . .

A deafening roar, a wave of darkness sweeps down on them. They're gone.

Lower Down the Mountain

Some time later. GRIZZLY's head torch, a faint glow off the ice.

GRIZZLY *is crumpled on a ledge. At the other end is the body of a dead climber.*

This is a different body. It's his brother's body.

GRIZZLY *stirs, struggling to sit up. The wind has died down. He has lost one ice boot.*

He sees the body of the climber at the other end of the ledge.

GRIZZLY. Told you . . . told you we'd do it.

Piece of piss . . . piece of fucking piss . . . Should have kept . . . going last time, man . . . breezed it . . .

You haven't got a fag on you, have you?

Thought not.

(*Rambling.*) So . . . What can you tell me, Pete? You been all right up here . . . ?

Thing is, we've got a great view from up here. Look on the bright side.

Pause.

Did you see the other guy, Pete? Did you? Up the hill a wee bit there . . . You been talking to him . . . ? He's got some weird ideas . . .

A paper dragon. I could see that, that could be handy up here, a dragon. Something to warm your hands on. Tell you what we need, a soup dragon.

An ice dragon. That's more likely, eh? Still . . . as long as it had wings. And a mountain, a picture of a mountain. Who brings a picture of a mountain onto a mountain?

Someone who really loves mountains maybe.

I don't. I hate the fuckers but here we are again.

Here we are again.

Another body becomes visible, a little lower down. It's DOG. GRIZZLY *doesn't see him.*

That's OK. That's OK, isn't it, Pete? The two of us, here. Were you waiting on me?

How're your feet, Pete? Still cold?

Cold.

Dark.

That's it.

That's our lot, eh?

That's no very fucking cheery, is it? What else is there Pete? Keep my spirits up, will you? It's dark. We're so small here in the dark on this mountain of ice. I don't mind. I don't mind being small here with you.

(*He sees* DOG.) Who's that?

Is that . . . Dog? No like him to be lying about. You watch. He'll be up in a minute. Never stops moving.

He better not stop moving, Pete. No safe.

(*Calling.*) Get moving, Dog!

Someone should get over there. Keep him warm.

You want to go, Pete? Don't think I'm fit for it.

Pause.

I'm not fit for anything else, am I, man? Might as well stop here. Going to stop here, Pete.

GRIZZLY *pats the body next to him.*

I won't leave you, man, I'll never leave you again.

Beside him the body of the climber jerks, it moves, it peels open.

The skeletal OLD MAN *from the hospital corridor climbs out of the climber's body as if it was a suit of clothes and stands on the ledge, looking at* GRIZZLY.

The sound of laboured breathing is very loud.

GRIZZLY stares at him.

You're not Pete, are you?

The OLD MAN just watches him. Fighting for breath, GRIZZLY pulls himself up.

You're not Pete. Who are you?

DOG. Grizzly? Col . . . Don't leave me.

GRIZZLY lurches forward, pushing the OLD MAN off the mountain.

The OLD MAN falls into the dark without a sound. GRIZZLY nearly falls after him. He catches himself on the edge, fighting to stay on. A moment when it looks like he's lost for sure . . . then he pulls himself back up.

GRIZZLY lies unmoving for a moment then, very slowly, he starts to crawl back to DOG, his breath rasping.

GRIZZLY's head lamp flickers.

GRIZZLY. I'm . . . here, Dog . . . here . . .

GRIZZLY pulls his head torch off. It flashes on, arcing against the sky, then goes out. Time passes. The wind rises again. GRIZZLY curls round DOG, huddling.

A head torch appears below: GNOME climbing up. She makes her way to them.

GNOME. Oh you fuck . . . you fuck . . .

She's checking for a pulse, shaking GRIZZLY and DOG.

Come on . . . Come on, you bastards.

She's instantly working on the ropes, clipping them on.

You breathing? You better be breathing . . . I'll . . . kill . . . you if you're not . . . breathing . . .

DOG *stirs weakly.*

DOG. Love you too, Gnomey.

Fade lights on the climbers and the mountain. The wind builds again, deafening.

The sun rises over the summit of the mountain as the wind rages.

Hospital

Lights up on the camp, now reassembled into a hospital room. The WIDOW *is standing, looking out the window.*

GRIZZLY *is lying on a hospital bed. His hands are heavily bandaged. One leg is lying on top of the covers. He's lost a foot, he's staring at the bandaged stump.*

GRIZZLY. Hi.

WIDOW (*turning and smiling*). Hullo.

GRIZZLY. Me again.

WIDOW. Yes.

What do you remember?

GRIZZLY. About what?

WIDOW. Do you remember talking to me yesterday?

GRIZZLY *tries to remember.*

GRIZZLY. Did I say anything bad?

WIDOW. We told you where you were.

GRIZZLY. Right.

It's hospital, right?

WIDOW. Yes.

GRIZZLY. Good. Could have been worse.

WIDOW. We explained that you're making a very good recovery. You were suffering from dehydration and exposure.

GRIZZLY. Oh yeah . . . Got some drought on right enough.

WIDOW. You lost the top joint of three fingers on your left hand but none on your right. But we couldn't save your foot.

GRIZZLY. That was it. Knew I'd lost track of something.

Yes. Yes. I remember all of that.

WIDOW. Good. You're doing well.

GRIZZLY *stares at his leg.*

GRIZZLY. I can still feel the bastard.

WIDOW. You will.

GRIZZLY. Look.

WIDOW. What?

GRIZZLY. That was me wriggling my toes.

WIDOW. It'll be OK.

GRIZZLY. Oh aye, aye . . .

WIDOW. You'll be moving downstairs later today.

GRIZZLY. Is that good?

WIDOW. That's very good.

GRIZZLY. If you say so. I'll miss the view.

He looks at her.

How are you?

WIDOW (*smiles*). Just the same.

GRIZZLY. Oh. That's a shame.

WIDOW. Did you find him?

GRIZZLY. Yes.

He wasn't there.

WIDOW. You know the night I fell in love with him? One of
the first time's he stayed over he did the washing up in the
middle of the night. The way I was brought up, guys never
did the washing up, even other men I knew then . . . they'd
do it *with* you or they'd do it if you sighed . . . all that crap.
Dave just did it, in the middle of the night in his underwear,
really quietly so as not to wake me up. I came in and saw
him at the kitchen sink, lifting china and glass out of the hot
water and putting them down to dry so gently, as if they
might explode. He had really strong hands but really
delicate fingers. Then he saw me and he grinned as if I'd
caught him out. And we talked in the middle of the night
while he washed plates, about films, kids . . . God.
Whatever we were thinking about. I thought, this is
everything I could ever want. We were a team.

GRIZZLY. He's not here, darling.

Pause.

WIDOW. He is for me. (*Pause.*) How are you?

78

GRIZZLY *thinks about it.*

GRIZZLY. I'll live.

Pause.

WIDOW. That's good.

GRIZZLY. Aye.

WIDOW. I won't see you again, I don't . . .

GRIZZLY. You don't do downstairs.

WIDOW (*smiles*). No.

GRIZZLY. Well, I'll think of you up next the clouds. Give you
a wave.

WIDOW. Do that.

The WIDOW *leaves.*

GRIZZLY *is still staring at his stump.* GNOME *comes in
quietly and sits down beside him. She picks up a magazine
and goes on reading it.*

DOG *puts his head round the door. He's on crutches,
bandaged up.*

DOG. You're a legend.

GRIZZLY. Says who?

For an answer GNOME *raises the magazine she's reading
in the air.*

GNOME (*finding the page*). 'A first ascent of the north west
face by legendary Colin Ross and Jack Harrier.'

DOG. No legendary for me, you notice, and it was my route.

GRIZZLY. That was quick.

DOG. You've been out of it for weeks, man.

GNOME. I gave the interview.

GRIZZLY. Did you, pet?

GNOME (*still reading*). I was fantastic. I cried.

GRIZZLY. Good on you. I deserve Gnome tears. I'm touched.
Did we make the papers? Were we on News at Ten?

GNOME. Course not. Nobody died.

GRIZZLY (*to* DOG). You all right?

DOG. Yeah, yeah, you?

GRIZZLY. Aye great. Fine. Lovely. Bit strange, that's all.

DOG. You'll be fine.

GRIZZLY. Yeah, yeah.

DOG. Bit of a weird one.

GRIZZLY. For sure.

Pause.

Keep looking under the bed for it.

DOG. What?

GRIZZLY. The foot.

DOG. Oh right, right, fuck yeah . . . 'Where did I drop that?'

GRIZZLY. Probably left it in the pub.

DOG. Yeah, go back and get that later.

Pause.

We did it, Grizzly. We made the top.

GNOME. Took me to get you to the bottom though, didn't it?

DOG. Fuck off. I was a miracle on those ropes, shattered ankle, two broken ribs, I was still a bloody ballet dancer.

GRIZZLY. What was I doing?

DOG. Bleeding mostly.

Fuck man . . . we were lucky . . . We were so . . .

GRIZZLY. I'll call it lucky when I can get down the pub again.

GNOME. Dog's been.

GRIZZLY. Without me?

DOG. Well, you were just lying about, no use to man or beast . . .

GRIZZLY. Should have waited for me.

DOG. I asked, I begged . . . I put matches under your fingernails . . .

GRIZZLY *is looking at his bandaged fingers.*

GRIZZLY. Oh, that explains it.

You miss me, Dog?

80

DOG. I did.

GRIZZLY (*surprised and pleased*). You did?

Well, don't worry. I reckon we've paid our dues, this time next year you'll be back up there.

DOG. Yeah.

I don't know. We did it.

GRIZZLY. Aye?

DOG. So it's done now, isn't it?

GRIZZLY. So do another one.

Pause.

DOG. You know what you've got there?

GRIZZLY. What?

DOG. An honourable discharge.

GRIZZLY. I suppose.

DOG. I wouldn't mind that.

Pause.

Just wanted to say . . .

GRIZZLY. You don't need to say anything, man.

DOG. Thing is . . . I tried to tell the Gnome this. She thinks I'm deranged or . . .

GNOME (*still reading*). No. Just don't think it's real. So I don't think you should worry.

DOG. I saw something up there. I swear I did. And then, even when we were getting you down . . . I was so fucking edgy . . . like I was losing it or . . .

GRIZZLY. You're not losing it. Just . . . takes a wee while to get comfortable again.

GNOME. You were in pain. You were in shock.

DOG. Yeah.

GRIZZLY. You don't want to be too comfortable anyway, man. Not safe.

DOG. Didn't you see something?

GRIZZLY. It's just in your head.

Pause.

Just what's in your head.

GNOME (*ticking it off*). Three days climbing, not enough fluid, not enough oxygen . . . exhaustion, dehydration, hypothermia . . . A fall that should have killed you both . . .

DOG. Yeah, yeah, yeah, OK, just checking.

Thought it had killed you.

We were drawing lots for who'd give you mouth to mouth.

I thought Gnomey needed the experience but she doesn't do beards.

GNOME (*still reading*). I don't do beards with lumps.

DOG. Lumps are the best bits, chewy surprises.

GRIZZLY. Good to be here, guys. Thanks.

DOG. Any time.

GRIZZLY. So what you doing now, man?

DOG. Don't know really. (*Fidgets.*) Got a chance to go over to the States. Drag racing, Death Valley . . .

GRIZZLY. Serious?

DOG. Yeah, friend of that guy in Chamonix last year . . . he said he could hook me up . .

Or Mexico maybe . . . that's supposed to be wild . . .

Get the motorbike back on the road maybe . . .

GRIZZLY. Sounds good.

DOG. Going away for a while, anyway.

GRIZZLY. OK.

DOG. So you better be vertical when I get back.

GRIZZLY. Working on it.

Pause.

DOG. Brought you something . . .

DOG *looks round furtively then pulls a bottle out of his trouser leg.*

GRIZZLY. Aw, fucking excellent . . .

DOG. Get it under the sheet, man, quick . . .

82

They hide the bottle.

GRIZZLY. What is it?

DOG. I don't know, picked it up from Ward Three. Don't drink it out a plastic cup. It melts it.

GRIZZLY. Brilliant. Thanks, man.

DOG. See you later.

DOG leaves. GNOME goes on reading for a few moments.

GNOME. You're not seeing that nurse again, are you?

GRIZZLY. No. They're shifting me.

GNOME. I don't like her.

GRIZZLY. Don't you? Why not?

GNOME. Cold hands.

GRIZZLY. You don't have to sit there you know, Gnome.

GNOME. Yeah I do.

Anyway. Haven't got anything to do till next May.

GRIZZLY. What's happening next May?

GNOME. I've got most of the sponsorship together for a trip to Janak Himal.

Pause, then GRIZZLY starts to laugh.

GRIZZLY. *Have* you, pet?

GNOME. I have.

GRIZZLY. And you never told us this because . . . ?

GNOME. I'm choosy about who I climb with. Need to weigh things like that up very carefully.

So that's what I'm doing. How about you?

GRIZZLY. Who knows.

GNOME. I think there was a better way up your first, Gualong though.

GRIZZLY. Do you?

GNOME. Yeah. Go up the south ridge, traverse on the face, easy stretch to the top . . .

GRIZZLY *thinks.*

GRIZZLY. You fuck.

GNOME. You see it now, don't you? Thought I might have a go after I'm done on the others next season.

GRIZZLY. I'd like to see that.

GNOME. Knock it off in two days.

GRIZZLY. Yeah, it's an easier line, but does it have the class?

GNOME. Is it legendary?

GRIZZLY. No way.

GNOME. None.

GRIZZLY. Dog's chucking it in, isn't he?

GNOME. I think so.

Pause.

He doesn't really want to climb without you. And that . . . upset him.

GRIZZLY. Which bit?

GNOME. All of it. The dead.

GRIZZLY. Are you OK, Gnomey?

GNOME. I always knew they were up there. How do you feel?

Pause. GRIZZLY *thinks about it, surprise and deep relief.*

GRIZZLY. Like I've done enough.

GNOME. Doesn't get better than that.

GRIZZLY. It does not.

Pause. GRIZZLY *looks at his crippled leg.*

Things are going to change, Gnomey, that's for sure.

GNOME (*apparently absorbed in her magazine again*). Thing is, I'd need someone who knows the ropes to organise everything, maybe come along as base camp manager. Thought if you could be arsed getting out of bed by then you could probably manage that.

GRIZZLY. Are you offering me work?

GNOME. Well . . . maybe . . . You are planning on walking again, aren't you?

GRIZZLY. Aye.

GNOME. See how you feel.

GRIZZLY. See how it goes.

So would that make you my boss?

GNOME. Yeah. You'd have to watch out. I'd keep you on your toe. You better be ready to hop to it.

GRIZZLY *stares at her.* GNOME *turns a page.*

You know what you will be able to do though? Nick shoes from outside shops.

GRIZZLY. You're right. They just put out one.

GNOME. All you need.

GRIZZLY. Fuck me, there's always a bright side.

GNOME. You're a happy man.

GRIZZLY. And a legend.

GNOME. What's the first thing you're going to do when you get out of here.

GRIZZLY. Get pissed.

GNOME. That's the way to go.

End.

A Nick Hern Book

Long Time Dead first published in Great Britain as a paperback
original in 2006 by Nick Hern Books Limited, 14 Larden Road,
London W3 7ST

Long Time Dead copyright © 2006 Rona Munro

Rona Munro has asserted her right to be identified as
the author of this work

Cover design by Ned Hoste, 2H

Typeset by Country Setting, Kingsdown, Kent CT14 8ES
Printed in Great Britain by
Antony Rowe Ltd, Chippenham, Wiltshire

A CIP catalogue record for this book is available from
the British Library

ISBN   978 1 85459 972 8